Wedding Bliss on a BUDGET

Ethan Baron

Self-Counsel Press
(a division of)
International Self-Counsel Press Ltd.
USA   Canada

Self-Counsel Press acknowledges the financial support of the Government of Canada through the Canada Book Fund (CBF) for our publishing activities.

Printed in Canada.

First edition: 2015

Library and Archives Canada Cataloguing in Publication

Baron, Ethan, author
    Wedding bliss on a budget / Ethan Baron.

(Personal finance series)
Issued in print and electronic formats.
ISBN 978-1-77040-222-5 (pbk.).—ISBN 978-1-77040-986-6 (epub).—
ISBN 978-1-77040-987-3 (kindle)

    1. Weddings—Planning. I. Title. II. Series: Self-Counsel personal finance series

HQ745.B368 2015	395.2'2	C2014-908249-5
		C2014-908250-9

Self-Counsel Press
(a division of)
International Self-Counsel Press Ltd.

Bellingham, WA	North Vancouver, BC
USA	Canada

MIX
Paper from
responsible sources
FSC® C004071

Contents

10 Wedding Party Gifts

11 Invitations and Other Paper Products

12 Official Business

Download Kit

Checklists

Worksheets

Samples

Notice to Readers

Laws are constantly changing. Every effort is made to keep this publication as current as possible. However, the author, the publisher, and the vendor of this book make no representations or warranties regarding the outcome or the use to which the information in this book is put and are not assuming any liability for any claims, losses, or damages arising out of the use of this book. The reader should not rely on the author or the publisher of this book for any professional advice. Please be sure that you have the most recent edition.

Note: The fees quoted in this book are correct at the date of publication. However, fees are subject to change without notice. For current fees, please check with the court registry or appropriate government office nearest you.

Prices, commissions, fees, and other costs mentioned in the text or shown in samples in this book probably do not reflect real costs where you live. Inflation and other factors, including geography, can cause the costs you might encounter to be much higher or even much lower than those we show. The dollar amounts shown are simply intended as representative examples.

Acknowledgments

The author wishes to thank the following wedding-service providers for their invaluable, expert insights into the wedding process:

Stacy Able, owner of Stacy Able Photography, Columbus/Indianapolis, Indiana.

Peter Barnett, owner of Premiere Catering, Portland, Oregon.

Richard Kamphuys, owner of Ancient Hill Estate Winery, Kelowna, British Columbia.

Karen Latanville, head chef at Davidson's Country Dining, Innisfil, Ontario.

Francisco Machado, chef and owner of 9Catering Services, Emeryville, California.

Michael Shandro, owner of Shandro Photo, Edmonton, Alberta.

Stephanie and Karl Will, owners of Sweet Impressions Bakery and Café, Central City, Louisiana.

Special thanks for exceptional assistance to Christina Averkin, florist, owner of A Bud & Beyond, Incline Village, Lake Tahoe, Nevada.

Introduction

Most advice you may read about weddings tells you that balancing dreams with financial reality requires a lot of sacrifice. This book is going to show you, step by step, how to make your dreams come true at a cost you can afford, without sacrificing what matters.

Don't be persuaded by the multibillion-dollar industry that says you should hire a wedding planner. A wedding planner typically charges 10 to 20 percent of your budget, which means you have 10 to 20 percent less to spend on your wedding. It's no wonder the industry's worth billions — it takes a big bite out of wedding budgets! Wedding planners will advertise that they can get their clients wedding services for a reduced price, but clients may spend far more on the planners' fees than they save through any minor discounts. In some cases, planners receive referral fees from vendors, which ultimately leads to more money taken out of wedding budgets. Planners will tell you that they will make sure the service providers show up on the wedding day, but if you hire reputable vendors, there's no need for that because they'll be there, on time.

You may not realize it, but when it comes to planning a wedding for a reasonable cost, you know the basics already. In fact, you live them.

In Chapter 1, you will find the Seven Steps to an Affordable Dream Wedding, which are simple guiding principles you will apply to the planning process to make sure you spend your time effectively, and achieve your wedding vision while staying within your budget.

In the chapters that follow, you'll find a timeline that lays out exactly what you need to do and when you need to do it. To keep track at all times of what's to be done, you can use the checklists and worksheets provided in these pages or complete and print the ones in the download kit (see the end of this book for more information).

You will discover how to find the services that meet your needs, for the lowest possible price. This book will help ensure that your wedding day turns out exactly the way you want it. Since you will be dealing directly with wedding-service providers, you will have no need to hire an expensive, and unnecessary, wedding planner. The following pages covers every element of the planning, from finding wedding-service providers such as florists and photographers, to booking the venue and caterer, to signing contracts, and sourcing a wedding cake. It will keep you organized, on time, and within budget.

When sensible people — who don't have unlimited finances — plan important purchases, they shop around. They find what they like, evaluate quality, and compare prices. When they find what they want, at an affordable cost, they make the purchase.

In planning your wedding, you'll make a series of important purchases, to obtain the goods and services required for the event. You'll use shopping and buying methods you already know well through the process of day-to-day living.

Most of wedding planning involves obtaining the services of vendors, such as photographers, florists, music providers, caterers, and venue providers. Chapters 3 through 8 show you how to find the best vendors, how to approach them, how to negotiate with them, and ultimately, how to ensure you receive their very best services for their very best price.

The steps in this book will allow you to tailor the wedding to your wishes, keep the process — and the expenditures — under your control, and ensure all goes smoothly on your wedding day and beyond. Think beauty, joy, fun, love, and memories you'll treasure forever. Think big — and think small. You're on your way to a perfect, affordable wedding.

The Seven Steps to an Affordable Dream Wedding

The seven steps in this chapter make up the guiding principles over-seeing the effective and satisfying planning of this extremely important event. By applying these principles to every element of the wedding planning, you will be able to achieve your goal of having your dream wedding at an affordable price. For each of the major elements of your wedding, the following chapters' section headings show you which steps to directly apply, and how to apply them.

Each of the seven steps will help you with the others, preparing you to achieve a perfect whole, a wedding that lets you express your-self through your own creation of the event — by taking control of the process, and costs, on the way up to the big day. The steps hold the key to ensuring that not only does the planning go smoothly and cost-effectively, you will be able to tick off each item on each list with the confidence of controlling the process and keeping it on track.

1. Step 1: Visualize

Visualizing is a special step. This is where you sort out what matters, and what you really want from your wedding — and it's easy. Your main goal for your wedding day is simple: You want to have the time of your life, surrounded by the people who matter most. You want every guest to enjoy a wonderful experience they'll recall fondly in the years to come. And you want this wedding with maximum impact for the minimum price. You will use this clear vision of the wedding to guide you as you prepare and execute your planning tasks.

2. Step 2: Prioritize

You will apply Step 2 throughout the planning process to ensure that you get what you really want, for a reasonable cost. You will apply this principle to deciding which elements of the wedding are the most important to you and which receive the appropriate share of the budget. You will prioritize the scenes you want the photographer to capture. You will decide which is more important, the wedding party flowers or the reception centerpieces. By always having your priorities in mind, you'll keep the planning process running smoothly, and make sure you accomplish your goals.

3. Step 3: Strategize

Time and money are your two main commodities of concern. You have a time budget as well as a financial budget — you need to balance the wedding planning with the rest of your life. Strategizing is about finding the most time- and cost-effective ways of achieving your wedding goals. Use the modern technology you have at hand to maximize the efficiency of the planning process. By strategizing, you can delegate many tasks while being in control of final decision-making. In the following pages you will learn to negotiate with high-quality service providers, and create positive relationships with the people who will help make your dream wedding happen.

4. Step 4: Scrutinize

Scrutinizing is a vital principle for finding your wedding vendors, and contracting their services. You need to look closely at potential vendors to decide which ones will end up on your list of possibilities. You need to look even more closely at the vendors you decide you'd like to hire, checking references to see how they performed for other clients. You need to examine your vendor contracts to make sure they describe in detail the exact products and services you require. The following pages will help you find the right vendors for your event, and how to evaluate them as well as what you must include in your vendor contracts.

5. Step 5: Minimize

This is not a time to ask, "What should our wedding include?" This is a time to ask, "What *must* our wedding include?" This is an easy question to answer because it's based on your priorities: What's most important to you as a couple, and to your family and friends who will be with you on your wedding day. You're not going to be cutting corners. You're going to be focusing on the essentials, and ensuring that you come away from your wedding day having had the experience you dreamed of, without burdening yourselves with debt.

6. Step 6: Maximize

Step 6 is a companion to Step 5. This is where you get the bang for your buck, and where you maximize the impact of every element of your wedding. You will learn how to keep costs down while keeping quality up, from securing customized contracts with talented photographers, caterers, and florists, to finding ceremony and reception venues that will provide appealing and memorable surroundings for your event. Paint your wedding with flourishes of beauty, and create a color palette that will express your personal taste and unify the elements of your wedding so that you can create a whole that captures the importance, excitement, and grandeur of your wedding day.

7. Step 7: Itemize

Itemizing is what this book is all about. You'll learn how to break down the wedding planning process according to your priorities and your strategies. By using the checklists and worksheets provided in this book (also included in the download kit), you can detail every step you need to take at every stage of the process, and the forms will allow you to keep track easily of every job that you need to accomplish. The forms cover everything you need to know before talking to wedding-service providers, the questions you need to ask, the clauses that need to go in contracts, and the overall wedding timeline that includes all your planning tasks.

Let's begin by looking at Checklist 1: The Wedding Planning Timeline. This checklist allows you to keep track easily of the entire wedding planning process. You'll be able to check boxes and write notes to mark your progress and stay on schedule. The chapters in this book will explain exactly what you need to do in order to tick off each item in this checklist.

Immediately after engagement:

[ ] Decide wedding date: _____

[ ] Decide ceremony time: _____

[ ] Decide reception time: _____

(If the ceremony and receptions are at different venues, remember to leave time between the ceremony and reception for transportation and photos, if required.)

[ ] Set your budget for the wedding: $_____

[ ] Write a breakdown of how much of the wedding budget will come from each source of funding.

    [ ] Confirm with funding sources, such as parents, how much they will provide, and for which components of the wedding event: _____

[ ] Schedule marriage counseling in accordance with religion, if applicable.

[ ] Select ceremony venue: _____

[ ] Select reception venue: _____

[ ] Select and book an officiant: _____

[ ] Choose and hire a photographer, make appointment for in-person meeting at least three months before wedding date: _____

[ ] Choose and hire a florist, make appointment for in-person meeting at least three months before wedding date: _____

[ ] Choose and hire a caterer (make sure you taste their cooking first!) or confirm alternative food and beverage plan: _____

Do the following at least six months before the wedding date:

[ ] Create the guest list.

[ ] Obtain addresses for all the guests that will be invited.

[ ] Send "save the date" cards or emails to people you are sure you will invite, giving them preliminary notice of your wedding and the date.

[ ] Arrange for accommodation for out-of-town guests:

    [ ] Arrange with a hotel for discounted rooms, if desired.

    [ ] Arrange with family and friends for accommodation in homes, if desired.

[ ] Book hotel, bed-and-breakfast, or other accommodation for bride and groom on wedding night, if required.

[ ] Compile a wish list for gift registry or registries.

    [ ] Set up gift registry or registries: _____

[ ] Decide on bridesmaids, if any, and confirm availability: _____

[ ] Decide on maid of honor and confirm availability: _____

[ ] Decide on groomsmen, if any, and confirm availability: _____

[ ] Decide on best man and confirm availability: _____

[ ] Decide on ushers, if any, and confirm availability: _____

[ ] Decide on ring bearer, and flower girl(s), if any, and confirm availability:

[ ] Buy wedding gown.

[ ] Choose bridesmaids' dresses and arrange that they are purchased.

[ ] Make appointments with hairstylist for a preliminary consultation and trial-run styling, and for wedding-day styling: _____

[ ] Make appointments with makeup artist for a preliminary consultation and trial-run makeup, and for wedding-day makeup: _____

[ ] Decide whether ceremony music will be live or a DJ: _____

[ ] Hire ceremony music provider: _____

[ ] Decide whether reception music will be live or a DJ: _____

[ ] Hire reception music provider: _____

[ ] Choose a baker and arrange for the wedding cake: _____

Do the following at least four months before the wedding date:

[ ] Provide preliminary guest numbers to caterer: _____

[ ] Book wedding day hairstyling for bridesmaids, or ensure bridesmaids make the booking, if desired: _____

[ ] Book wedding day makeup for bridesmaids, or ensure bridesmaids make the booking, if desired: _____

[ ] Find out what decor and utility items the caterer does not provide. This may include napkins and linens; any decorations beyond what the florist may provide for the venue, the guest book table, the dining tables, and the cake table; cake knife: _____

    [ ] Book rental of napkins and linens, if caterer does not provide them.

    [ ] Buy a cake knife, or arrange to bring or borrow one for the cake cutting.

[ ] Order cake.

[ ] Online: Create a wedding announcement, a wedding program, and a thank-you note, and order samples.

    [ ] Order wedding invitations, wedding programs, and thank-you notes upon receipt of satisfactory samples.

[ ] Choose a bridal shower date and location (between two months and two weeks before the wedding date): _____

[ ] Send bridal shower invitations.

[ ] Arrange for any required wedding-day transportation of the bride, groom, wedding party, and family members: _____

[ ] Order or obtain guest book.

[ ] Buy the ring pillow for the ceremony, if using.

[   ] Buy garter for bride, if planning on garter toss.

[   ] Make honeymoon plans: If pondering a foreign country, make sure you have valid passports (some countries will deny entry if the passport expires too closely to the end date of your trip):

    [   ] Book honeymoon flights or other transportation tickets.

    [   ] Book honeymoon lodging.

    [   ] Book honeymoon vehicle rental, if required.

    [   ] Buy travel health insurance and visas if necessary, if honeymooning outside the country.

Do the following at least three months before the wedding date:

[   ] Send wedding invitations.

[   ] Order wedding rings.

[   ] For a formal wedding: Ensure the outfits of the mothers of the bride and groom are coordinated. (By tradition, the bride's mom chooses first, and the groom's mom selects something that will complement it.)

[   ] Meet the photographer to discuss goods and services, and prepare a contract.

[   ] Meet the florist to discuss goods and services, and prepare a contract.

[   ] Buy or reserve for rental the groom's suit or tuxedo.

[   ] Arrange for groomsmen's suits:

    [   ] Groomsmen agree on using own suits, in color coordination.

    [   ] Groomsmen fitted for suit rental and rent suits.

[   ] Consult a lawyer about a prenuptial agreement, if any.

Do the following at least two months before the wedding date:

[   ] Confirm bridal shower attendees.

[   ] Buy shoes for bride.

[   ] Buy or arrange shoes for bridesmaids.

    [   ] Recommend bridesmaids break in any new shoes by wearing them at least two hours per week in the month before the wedding.

[   ] Buy gifts for wedding party.

[   ] Buy gifts for wedding-planning helpers.

[   ] Schedule a bridesmaids' lunch at your home, or at one of your bridesmaid's homes, to discuss the wedding planning, the plan for the wedding day, and additions to confirm:

    [   ] Wedding date, time, and location.

    [   ] Time and location for bridesmaids' wedding day preparation.

    [   ] Confirm the amount of time needed to get from the preparation location to the ceremony location.

[   ] Online: Create and order guest place cards for reception, if needed.

[ ] Choose, perhaps from among your bridal party or family, a helper or helpers to be responsible for the following:

    [ ] Ensuring cake(s) are brought to or delivered to reception.

    [ ] Ensuring cake knife is brought to or delivered to reception.

    [ ] Taking charge of gifts brought to the reception and/or ceremony.

    [ ] Putting out the guest book with pens, and retrieve it at the end of the reception.

    [ ] Setting out the guest table-assignment cards in alphabetical order.

[ ] Designate a person, not in the wedding party, who will handle any issues that come up on the wedding day, and who will keep track of the helpers: _____

[ ] Find out what the marriage license requirements are for the jurisdiction in which you will marry:

    [ ] Get blood tests, if required.

    [ ] Ensure you have all required documents.

[ ] Sign prenuptial agreement, if any.

Do the following by at least one and a half months before the wedding date:

[ ] Contact invitees who have not responded to confirm if they are coming.

Do the following at least 30 days before the wedding date:

[ ] Confirm with the caterer (or the venue if it's doing the catering) the final number of attendees, as well as event time, date, and services. Note that your caterer may have a different deadline, and will inform you as to the required date for the final count.

[ ] Final fittings, if required, for bride's and bridesmaids' dresses.

[ ] Confirm time, date, and services with the following:

    [ ] Photographer.

    [ ] Videographer, if any.

    [ ] Venue.

    [ ] Florist (including exact number of tables for centerpieces, and number of chair rows at ceremony for any decor there).

    [ ] Music provider.

[ ] Arrange rehearsal dinner.

[ ] Create seating map for reception.

[ ] Apply for marriage license.

[ ] Keep a record of gifts as they are received, including shower gifts, and who they are from.

[ ] Send thank-you cards for any gifts already received.

[ ] Bride and groom should start wearing wedding-day shoes, if new, around the house for at least two hours per week.

Do the following at least two weeks before the wedding date:

[   ] Give final guest count to caterer.

[   ] Confirm date and location of rehearsal dinner with those who will attend.

[   ] Confirm date and location of rehearsal dinner with vendors such as caterer and venue, if any.

[   ] Confirm time and location where bride and bridesmaids will get ready on the wedding day.

[   ] Confirm wedding day transportation for bride and groom, family members, and wedding party.

[   ] Confirm parking arrangements for ceremony (ensure any guests with disabilities are provided for).

[   ] Confirm parking arrangements for reception (ensure any guests with disabilities are provided for).

Do the following at least one week before the wedding date:

[   ] Touch base with the person you've designated to handle any issues on the wedding day, and discuss the status of the wedding planning and any potential issues.

[   ] Confirm honeymoon arrangements:

    [   ] Tickets.

    [   ] Accommodation.

    [   ] Vehicle rental.

    [   ] Pack for honeymoon.

Do the following one day before the wedding date:

[   ] Hold rehearsal dinner.

[   ] Touch base with anyone who's helping out during wedding day events and confirm arrangements including timing (you may be able to do this at your rehearsal dinner).

[   ] Give bridesmaids and groomsmen their gifts.

[   ] Give to the best man the rings, marriage license, and any payment for officiant, or clergy fees.

Do the following the day of the wedding:

[   ] Ensure designated helpers, including ushers, are prepared for their tasks.

[   ] Bride has her hair and makeup done.

[   ] Bridesmaids have their hair and makeup done.

[   ] Bridal party begins dressing two hours before the time they have to leave for the ceremony.

[   ] Groom and groomsmen begin dressing one hour before they have to leave for the ceremony.

2
Your Wedding Budget and Guest List

Your wedding budget has a number of elements that make up the total cost. However, one element carries the largest potential price, and offers the easiest way to save money: The guest list. The number of guests governs the cost of two of the more expensive elements of your wedding, the venue(s), and the catering. The more guests you have, the bigger the ceremony and reception venues must be; and the more meals and refreshments you must provide.

This chapter will provide you with guidance and a concrete method for addressing your guest numbers. However, from the start of your wedding planning, keep in mind that you can have the greatest impact on your overall wedding costs by inviting only guests you determine are essential. As you'll see, when you apply a method to the task, it's not as hard as it may seem!

1. Preparing Your Wedding Budget

Most of your wedding costs will go to vendors, including the venue. Typically, catering and venue costs will make up the greatest portion of the budget; however, this is not an ironclad rule. Different brides and grooms have varying priorities for the major elements of the wedding. By ranking these elements by how important they are to you,

you'll be prepared to create your budget. Remember that you may find, for example, that although flowers and music are higher priorities for you than the food, you can't escape allocating more of the budget for catering.

1.1 Prioritize: Ranking your vendors

Your ranking will guide you as you decide how much money will be allocated to each element of the wedding. While a typical wedding budget breakdown exists, you need to create your own to match your priorities and to reflect the savings you plan to achieve for each element of the wedding.

Typically, the venue, catering, and cake total 50 percent of the expenses. Clothing, flowers and decoration, photography and videography, and music are allocated to 10 percent each. The other 10 percent is made up half by invitations and other paper products, and wedding gifts and favors. However, many couples choose to break down their spending quite differently, perhaps emphasizing flowers and photography, or the venue, music, and food.

In Checklist 2, number the ranking spaces from 1 to 6, according to how important they are to you. There may be other elements you would like to add to the list as well.

Worksheet 1
Rank Your Vendors

Rank	Element
	Venue
	Photographer
	Florist
	Catering
	Music
	Clothing for the bride and groom
	Other:
	Other:
	Other:

1.2 Minimize: Your wedding party

Which people you choose to have standing beside you as you enter into marriage can be hugely important. However, if you have trouble keeping the numbers of bridesmaids and groomsmen reasonable, the costs will add up. Each requires a bouquet or a boutonniere. Each requires a wedding party gift.

It has become traditional for bridesmaids and groomsmen to pay for their own wedding day attire, and hairstyling for bridesmaids, with the wedding couple showing their gratitude with wedding party gifts. However, circumstances vary among couples and their wedding parties, and financial constraints among bridesmaids and groomsmen may have to be addressed. No bride and groom want to place an undue financial burden on those who are committing to stand beside them on their important day. Some couples offer to pay part of the cost of the attire. Others leave the dress purchases up to the bridesmaids but pay for accessories and/or hairstyling themselves. It's also becoming increasingly popular for bridesmaids to wear different, but coordinated, outfits that either already belong to them or are of a style that can be worn on other occasions in the future.

In weddings for which the bride and groom pay the costs of the wedding party attire, gifts to wedding party members are not necessary, but of course a nice thank-you note for playing a key role in the wedding is obligatory.

As with creating your guest list, deciding on wedding party members can be challenging, and fraught with interpersonal peril. If you have many close friends, how do you choose? Do you include family members? Keeping your wedding party small is a very good way to keep your costs lower. Use Worksheet 2 to create your wedding party list; you can add more names by using the form provided in the download kit.

1.3 Itemize: Budget and deposits

This is where the math calculations begin. Don't worry; it's simple stuff — a percentage game. Calculate what percentage of your budget will go to which of the major elements of the wedding. Don't forget to budget 5 percent for miscellaneous costs. For each element in Worksheet 3, multiply the percentage you've allocated to it by the total wedding budget, and fill in the blanks. You can also use the worksheet to keep track of when deposits to vendors and the venue(s) are due, how much you need to pay, and what method of payment you will use. Check off the item in the "Deposit Paid" column when you have paid your deposit. There is also a final column that you can check when you have paid the rest of the balance.

Worksheet 2
Wedding Party List and Contact Information

Name	Cell Phone Number	Email Address
Maid of Honor:		
Bridesmaids:		
1.		
2.		
3.		
Best Man:		
Groomsmen:		
1.		
2.		
3.		

2. Preparing Your Guest List

Preparing the guest list can be the hardest part of the whole planning process, but there's no cause for despair. It's the single highest-impact wedding element to economize. Guest numbers are the largest individual component of the entire wedding price, because each guest increases the costs in the major expense areas — venue and catering.

The more guests you have, the bigger the venue you need, and the higher the price you are likely to pay. More guests means more floral arrangements for reception tables, and more meals and drinks to pay for to the caterer. Reducing your guest list is not only the single biggest-impact method for reducing overall costs, but it allows you to cut expenses without affecting the overall wedding experience.

Picking the people you'd like to have at your wedding is easy. Picking the people you *must* have at your wedding is more difficult.

Worksheet 3
Budget the Major Elements

Total Wedding Budget: $_____							
Vendors/ Items	Budget Percentage	Deposit Amount	Deposit Due Date	Deposit Paid	Method of Payment	Total Due after Deposit Paid	Total Paid
Venue: Ceremony							
Venue: Reception							
Photographer							
Florist							
Catering							
Music							
Baker							
Clothing for bride							
Clothing for groom							
Miscellaneous costs:							

The guest list can be tricky, and fraught with family peril. Here's one simple principle to operate by, and if you stick to this principle, you can make sure to create an event filled with people you cherish and value, while you strike your biggest blow against costs: *Invite only people whose attendance is essential to a current relationship that you value.*

Here's how to apply this principle: Rule out every potential guest whom you could decline to invite without damaging an important relationship.

Now you can apply this principle to each category of guest such as family members, friends, and work-related associates. It must be remembered that the pool of potential guests also includes friends, significant others, and associates of family members, friends, and workmates.

Choosing family members is the easy part. You invite the family members you are close to; the ones you see regularly, or maintain strong relationships with from a distance.

Of key importance here is limiting the numbers of family members' companion guests. If your married cousin is invited, her husband should be, too. If your aunt is in a long-term relationship, her partner needs to be invited, too. As for your cousin's new boyfriend, or your aunt's new girlfriend? This is where you have to draw some lines. You do this by applying the relationship-based principle. You love your cousin, and adore your aunt, but if you tell them you want their company only, with no second guest, will this cause lasting damage to your relationship? In most cases, the answer is no.

Choosing friends is the hardest part. You want every one of your friends at your wedding. If you had unlimited finances, that would be possible. But one of the reasons you're holding this book is because you want to keep costs reduced. You want your important friends to be there. So, on the big day, whom can you live without? To answer that question, apply the relationship principle. Will you still have the relationship you want with a particular friend if you don't invite him or her to your wedding? Then there's the slightly touchy matter of companions. Here, as with family, you apply the standard: Is your friend in a long-term, committed relationship with the potential companion? If the answer is yes, and your friend wishes to have his or her companion accompany him or her, you should invite the companion.

Worksheet 4 will help you keep track of the guest list and RSVPs. By using Worksheet 4 in the download kit, you can add as many lines as you need.

Worksheet 4
Guest List

Name	Address	Phone Number	RSVP Sent Yes/No	Attending Yes/No	Number of Guests Attending

2.1 Minimize: Note to parents

We must, for a moment, address the parents and close family of the bride and groom.

The wedding event should be shaped by the couple at its center. It should be a celebration of their love and togetherness. On their special day, the bride and groom want to be surrounded by two types of people: close family, and close friends. It's these people — beyond the venue, flowers music, food, and photos — that will create the memories for all who attend, and who will give to the couple the knowledge that their union has been shared with the people in their lives who are truly important. The focus should stay on the bride and groom.

Parents, if you want to see the most beautiful wedding possible for a cost that doesn't burden anyone in the family, do your very best to reduce the number of guests you invite for yourselves. If you need to invite one or two close friends or important business associates, by all means do so. However, you can help the bride and groom make their challenging decisions about the guest list much easier, and help them reduce costs, by cutting down on the guests that you add to the list.

2.2 Visualize: Guest wedding favors

You can cover the wedding favor base inexpensively and easily through some Internet shopping and a few minutes of your time. Options abound for small favors your guests will appreciate finding at their reception place settings, which won't take a big bite out of your budget.

With some choices, you can order them personalized, or order personalized tags to attach to them, but this can add to the cost. The following list provides you with some inexpensive ideas for wedding guest favors:

- Personalized wildflower seed packets are a gift of future beauty for your guests, and start at around 30 cents each.

- You can buy colorful, sheer organza bags for about 10 cents each, put a few Jordan almonds or mints in each, tie them up, and they're ready to go.

- Small paper bags with personalized text and imagery also make great containers for wrapped candies, mints, or Jordan almonds, and go for about 50 cents apiece.

- Wrapped candies, personalized with the couple's names or a favorite saying can be purchased for between 25 cents and 50 cents each.

- Bubble bottles, or bubble tubes, can be bought for less than 25 cents, with personalized versions costing a bit more.

- Personalized matches range in price from around 15 cents for matchbooks, to 50 cents for boxes.

- Miniature picture frames usually cost $1 to $2, and provide guests with a useful keepsake from your wedding.

- Personalized frosted-glass votive candle holders will also serve your guests as a pretty, and useful memento, and cost about $2 each.

- Tiny succulent plants are in vogue for wedding floral designs, and also make for appealing wedding favors, costing about $1.50 each.

2.3 Itemize: Guest accommodation

Couples expecting guest from out of town usually make hotel arrangements. Often, discounted rates can be obtained for guests to the wedding. If you have out-of-town guests, consider contacting local accommodation providers and asking if they can set aside rooms for your guests, at a discounted room rate.

Working with the Vendors

We live in fortunate times for those, like you, who are planning their own wedding. Never in history has it been easier to find the professionals who will provide your wedding services. These are the vendors — florist, caterer, photographer, music provider, dress supplier, and venue provider.

Wedding service providers are people, and when you're working with them, relationships matter. How you work with your wedding vendors has a tremendous impact on the quality of service you receive. You don't just want their work; you want them to do their very best job at it. By treating vendors well from your initial contact with them — being friendly, polite, and returning phone and email messages promptly — you create a positive professional relationship that will see the vendors putting in their best effort. The stakes are high for you, because, after all, you're getting married, and emotions and worries may arise at times when you're working with vendors, but if you pick the right ones, you'll have little cause for concern because ultimately you trust them to do their job.

You want to hire vendors you like, personally, and enjoy dealing with. It's a professional relationship. It should be based on respectful, clear communication about what you want and can afford, and what the vendor can provide, at what price. But it should also be fun for everyone involved.

1. Maximize: Your Search for Vendors

In Chapter 2, Worksheet 1, you ranked the importance of each type of vendor. Now, you will need to do your research to create a list of your Top 5 contenders in each vendor category. The Internet enables you to cast a wide net among providers of wedding services. Rank your vendor options in order of preference. Keep in mind, you may find you have to rework your Top 5 lists in the initial stages because once you start contacting vendors, you may discover that they are either unavailable or their prices are beyond the reach of your budget.

Spend a few minutes on the Internet, or leafing through wedding magazines, and you can find pictures from spectacular weddings. You can see bridal gowns priced for princesses, floral decor more expensive than a new vehicle, meals fit for royalty, and photographs taken by the best wedding photographers in the world. Beware of the "Media Effect"! Although you can, and should, draw inspiration from the lovely designs, goods, and pictures that you see, keep firmly in mind that what you're looking at, in many cases, is very expensive to produce.

Some vendors list their prices on their websites, and you can tell right away if they're an option for you. Often, you'll be calling or emailing vendors to ask preliminary questions about their availability, prices, and willingness to make customized arrangements. To be able to quote you a price, the vendors need to know exactly what you're looking for and the date you need their services.

Here's your goal: You want the best possible goods and services for the lowest possible price.

Here's your strategy: Find high-quality vendors who charge a range of prices, depending on what they provide. Find out about vendors' lower-priced options, and choose vendors whose less-expensive offerings meet your needs.

You, and any people who are helping you, are not looking for top-secret information. Wedding-service vendors do everything they can to make it easy for people to find them on the Internet. Many venues have lists of "recommended" vendors, who may or may not meet your needs and budget. Names of vendors on those lists can be considered along with the names you find through your research.

Get help by contacting friends and family, asking if they know of any wedding florists, caterers, photographers, music providers, or venues they can recommend, preferably with website links. You'll save yourself research time and you may find high-quality vendors who have connections to your circle and are more amenable to flexible pricing arrangements. If you have friends or family members who know your taste, and understand your budget, ask them if they could do you a wedding-planning favor and conduct some research for a particular element of the wedding, such as the photographer, caterer, or florist.

Is your cousin married to a photographer? Does your mother's friend own a catering company? You may find you have connections to vendors who will offer their services for a reduced rate because of that connection. Remember, you want professionals who will show up on time and do a professional job. There are lots of enthusiastic amateur photographers, and plenty of good home-kitchen cooks, but hiring an amateur can turn out disastrously. You must evaluate the reliability and quality of personally connected potential vendors as rigorously as you evaluate the vendors with whom you have no connection.

Review everything on the vendor's website. For example, if you are looking at a photographer's website, look at his or her portfolios and galleries presented on the site. If you like the photographer's work, check to see if there are prices posted so you can right away rule out any vendors who are too expensive.

Add a bookmark for each vendor whose website makes it a "possible." When you have 10 options, return to each website and narrow the list down to five. Put those five vendors on the Top 5 list such as Worksheet 5 (you can print as many copies as you need by using the form in the download kit). Follow the same search process for each type of vendor as you read through the related chapters.

Use online review websites such as Yelp to get an idea of how a vendor has performed. **Caution:** Such websites must be taken with a grain of salt. Vendors may receive the occasional bad review from someone who had no valid reason for reviewing the vendor poorly. Vendors may pose as clients, and write up stellar reviews. On some review websites, vendors are given prominence if they buy advertising on the site.

Also, as part of your investigation into potential vendors, run them through the general search function on the Better Business Bureau's website. Don't use the bureau's search function for accredited businesses because the vendor you're looking into may not be accredited. Keep in mind that many upstanding businesses aren't accredited by the bureau. The general search function will help you find out if your vendor has a history of complaints from customers, and how the bureau rates it, based on factors including length of time in operation, complaints, and adherence to licensing requirements.

Worksheet 5
Top 5 Vendor Choices

Vendor Type: _____			
Vendor Name	**Phone Number**	**Contacted**	**Quote**
1.			
2.			
3.			
4.			
5.			

1.1 Strategize: Off-season and off-peak savings

Many venues, caterers, photographers, and music providers charge premium rates during the high season for weddings. That season varies geographically, according to how long winter lasts and how hot summers get (though December is popular across North America, because people get time off).

During off-peak dates and times, many vendors are more willing to accommodate customized arrangements involving more limited service. At times of peak demand for vendors' services, many will only accept full-service contracts for maximum goods and services. Consider the following:

- Scheduling your wedding in the off-season can bring considerable savings.

- Scheduling your wedding on an off-day of the week can also bring significant savings. Prices for venues and vendors are often highest on Saturday afternoons and evenings. Scheduling your wedding for midweek, Friday, or Sunday can reduce costs across the board.

- Reducing catering costs considerably by having a morning wedding ceremony with a reception brunch to follow. This increasingly popular option is far less expensive than a sit-down dinner reception, and the guests have a great time. Alcohol costs can be significantly lower for a brunch reception.

Be mindful of potential weather challenges for off-season weddings. Winter weather can cause transportation problems that affect not only wedding party members and guests, but vendor services as well. Rain can disrupt plans for outdoor ceremonies and receptions, and make preferred outdoor portrait photography locations unavailable. Severe heat can affect the comfort and health of wedding participants and guests.

1.2 Itemize: The Vendor Contact List

Once you have decided on a vendor, record its contact information. In Chapter 2, Worksheet 3, you can record the deposit, due date, and final balance to be paid.

Worksheet 6 will help you stay organized and have easy access to all your vendors contact information. With each vendor, ask for a cell phone number so you can contact them easily and reliably. Keep in mind that when contacting vendors during hours they may be working it may be more effective to make contact by text message. List email addresses for vendors as well. Ensure that all vendors have your email address and cell phone number as well as a cell phone number for a person who will be at all your wedding events and can be called as an alternative to you.

2. Strategize and Scrutinize: Custom Vendor Contracts

Most vendors have boilerplate contracts that cover the basics of what they will provide, and include legal language that protects them from liability. This contract is written to meet the vendor's needs, not necessarily the client's. It may not even have space for specific vendor obligations to the client. There's nothing wrong with using this type of contract as a base, but to make sure you have legal documentation of exactly what you are purchasing for the agreed-upon price, your contract with each vendor must contain all the details of what they will be providing for you. You want a contract that clearly defines the vendor's responsibilities to you as a client, and have the vendor's responsibilities in writing. Don't be afraid to ask vendors to modify or add to a contract, even if their standard form doesn't provide space for customizations. An additional page or two may be required. For example, your contract with the florist must specify the exact number of bouquets, boutonnieres, and centerpieces the florist will provide. Your contract with the photographer must detail the elements of the wedding day to be photographed, and the locations for photography, and the hours of service. In the following chapters, there are contract checklists for each major vendor so you can make sure all necessary bases are covered in your contracts. The contract not only provides legal protections to you and the vendor, it helps ensure the exact arrangements are understood and agreed on by you and the vendor.

Worksheet 6
Vendor Contact List

Vendors/Items	Contact Person	Cell Phone Number	Business Phone Number	Email Address	Vendor Address
Venue: Ceremony					
Venue: Reception					
Photographer					
Florist					
Catering					
Music					
Transportation					
Clothing for bride					
Clothing for groom					
Baker					
Other:					

You also need to know what your budget is for each vendor. In some cases, you will be negotiating customized arrangements, and ordinarily in negotiations over a purchase, a car for example, you wouldn't want to reveal what your budget is. Some wedding-service vendors won't be able to work for you because your budget is too small. All of them will need to know what they can provide for you, based on how much you have to spend. You, and they, won't be able to figure that out until you let them know what your budget is for their services. Once you start discussing services and prices, there's room for you to negotiate.

Being up front with vendors about your budget will save you valuable time. When you're seeking to make customized arrangements with vendors to suit your budget, often the best approach is to tell them how much you have to spend, and ask what they can do for you for that price. Listen to their ideas about what they can do within your budget. The key here is to work with reputable vendors who will provide you the value you're paying for, not vendors who will see your budget as a golden goose ripe for the squeezing.

Shop around and ask for quotes so you can get a clear idea of what the going rate is for what you want. You'll get a preliminary idea of which vendors you feel can best fit your needs. Keep in mind that it's always in a vendors' best interest to maximize their own profit — even good ones, who practice business fairly, may try to up-sell. Don't be afraid to resist sales pressure and negotiate assertively.

You will be signing contracts with each vendor. It's important to remember that a typical service contract protects the vendor as much as possible from financial liability in case something goes wrong — including situations in which the vendor, through negligence, fails to deliver the legally agreed on products and services. This is typical in such legal agreements. This is why proper screening of your chosen vendor is so essential.

There are incompetent operators out there, and vendors struggling unsuccessfully to run a business that turns a profit. Just in case, you should make vendor payments with a credit card in the event that something goes wrong and you need to cancel or contest the payment. Be advised that some reputable vendors don't accept credit cards. Contracts must spell out a cancellation policy that details the amount of deposit or payment you lose if you cancel the contract. Contracts must also contain a refund policy covering the amount you are entitled to receive should the vendor cancel the contract or fail to do the work.

Throughout the planning process, you'll be communicating with vendors by phone and email. To make the most of your time, pick your best communication skill — by phone or email — and use that the most.

Often a quick phone call with a brief discussion about what you're looking for and what prices and services a vendor offers, is the most efficient way to sort out whether a vendor makes your Top 5 list. You can get an idea of the vendors' professionalism and reliability by how quickly they reply to emails and phone messages. You'll be confirming specifics such as price and services to be offered later, after you've narrowed down the list of your Top 5.

In hiring your wedding vendors, a bit of preparation is key to ensuring the process goes smoothly, quickly, and effectively. First, unless you're setting your wedding date based on the availability of a particular venue or vendor, you'll need to know when you're getting married. Your first question to every vendor should be, "Are you available on my wedding date?" If the answer is "No," move on to the next choice on your list.

If the answer is "Yes," your next question will be, "What is your price for the goods and/or services I require?" To be able to ask that question, you must be able to tell each wedding-service provider what you want to hire them for, and exactly which goods and services you require, from the photographer's list of specific shots, to the number of bouquets, boutonnieres, and centerpieces, to the colors and varieties that will be in the bride's bouquet.

Now, the saying "too many cooks" can apply across the board in your wedding planning, and not just for catering. Involvement of additional people in the planning process makes it more complicated and slows it down — just what you don't need! Pressure from family members and friends to make particular choices about vendor services — from food selection, to flowers, to the wedding dress — can lead to increased costs.

The following pages will provide you with information, checklists, and worksheets dedicated to each major vendor so you can make sure you cover all the bases in every stage from the search for vendors, to signing the contract, to the day of your wedding.

Finding the Venue That Is Right for Your Wedding

Your venue options are limitless, and so are your options for saving money. Here, you can find tremendous benefits by thinking outside the box; creative thinking will bring you to a venue that will be memorable, and affordable.

1. Maximize: Options for Venues

To begin, you must decide whether you'll marry in a house of worship, or another type of wedding ceremony venue. You must also decide where you'll hold your reception. Often, you can save a significant amount of money if you hold the ceremony and reception at the same site.

Before deciding on a venue, you'll have to come up with an approximate guest count, so you can ensure the venue is neither too small, nor too large.

Keep in mind that venue prices are usually lower in the off-season (usually November, and January through April, although it varies geographically), on days other than Saturday, and sometimes at off-hours, such as mornings and early afternoons.

In and around your community, or the area in which you plan to marry, a multitude of possibilities arise. Marrying in a church may be more economical than in a private venue such as a hotel ballroom or hall, particularly if one or both of the couple are congregants at the church. As an added benefit, many churches designate volunteer helpers who help with the arrangements, and may manage a rehearsal — although there is sometimes a fee for that service.

Costs associated with church weddings vary. Catholic churches require donations at the couple's discretion. Other churches charge specific fees for the pastor, the wedding host, music services, and custodial services. It's not uncommon for church fees for a wedding to total around $500, but the price can be lower depending on the couple's connection to the church.

Synagogue facility fees for weddings vary from nominal charges to thousands of dollars, depending on the location. The rabbi's honorarium and the traditional wedding canopy (the chuppah) can add at least $1,000, although many rabbis are somewhat flexible on their fees.

Ballrooms in posh hotels can cost thousands of dollars to rent, or require you to spend thousands on catering in exchange for use of the space. Note that costs are higher in major metropolitan areas. However, mid-range hotels often offer ballroom space starting at about $200 for a 50-person wedding reception. Almost always, however, hotels require you use their in-house catering for any meals and beverages to be served, which can add a great deal to your total costs.

Many non-traditional venues have the added benefit of allowing you to use the caterer of your choice, and supply your own alcoholic beverages, which can reduce costs significantly. If a venue does not supply furniture, rental costs can eat up some venue-related savings.

When making initial inquiries about venue availability and prices, avoid disclosing that you wish to book the space for a wedding, as some venues automatically charge a higher price. A "family event" is enough description during initial contact, and make sure you note the quoted price and confirm it and the name and position of the person you've contacted. Be mindful that most venues impose overtime charges if your event runs past the scheduled end, and venue staff must stay longer. Some also impose cleanup charges, and fees for music performance.

Although many venues have non-negotiable set prices, smaller venues such as studios and wineries may be open to some negotiation. If the price is not set, keep your budget to yourself. This is a different situation from negotiating a variety of goods and services with photographers, florists, and caterers. Hiring a venue is not a customized arrangement that requires you and a vendor to sort out prices, possibilities, and impossibilities regarding a variety of goods and services. There's no need to reveal to a venue representative how much you have to spend.

Be sure to take a look at the parking available at your venue(s) to make sure there will be adequate parking for your guests.

The following sections discuss some more options for venues.

1.1 Home and/or yard

Does one of your family members — perhaps the bride's or groom's parents — have a lovely house and yard where the wedding could take place? This venue has the virtue of familial closeness, and the financial benefit of costing nothing. Similarly, a friend of the bride and groom, or a friend of the family, may be happy to have the wedding, and reception, at their home. Keep in mind that holding a wedding and/or reception in a private home can require expenditures for tables, chairs, lighting, and catering.

Also, make sure to account for bathroom requirements. If an informal venue such as a home has only one bathroom, and guest numbers require additional facilities, you will need to rent portable bathrooms, and portable sinks for washing up.

1.2 Public spaces

A public amenity may work for you, such as a beach, park, garden, art gallery, museum, community center, clubhouse, museum, or historical site. Many such venues have boundless charm and beauty, and can be booked for a wedding ceremony for the price of the required permits. Some locations can also be used for the reception.

Some libraries rent event spaces, and can provide a comfortable site for ceremonies and receptions, especially appealing to couples with a literary bent.

Community facilities, whether in a private development or a public space, often have open outdoor areas, and large indoor areas. They may also have outdoor and indoor seating and tables, and sometimes have kitchen facilities.

A private art gallery or artist's studio may also work for you. An art gallery or studio can provide a lovely, well-lit site for a wedding — a setting that attendees will remember.

1.3 Bed and breakfast

Many bed and breakfasts have picturesque yards, and comfortable indoor areas, for ceremonies and receptions. Also, the bride and groom, and out-of-town guests, have an excellent accommodation option for the night of the wedding.

1.4 Restaurant

A favorite restaurant, or one you find attractive, that's of sufficient size for your event, can provide an excellent venue for a reception, and take care of the food and refreshments, possibly at a much lower cost than you might otherwise pay separately for a venue and a caterer.

If you choose the restaurant option, you will likely be prohibited from bringing in outside food and drink. Any violation of this prohibition — even by guests carrying liquor flasks — can draw a very strong response from a restaurant owner or manager who may feel cheated, and could shut down the party! However, serving of outside food and drink can be negotiable, depending on the restaurant. Some allow clients to bring in their own bar service, or even catering, for additional fees, but such an arrangement must be negotiated and written into the contract.

1.5 Winery or Brewery

By choosing a winery for your wedding, you've automatically immersed yourself in an age-old romance, and often in scenic beauty. Note that wineries come in all sizes. Famed vintners may rent space for weddings, at high prices, but smaller winemakers, whose facilities will likely possess all the classic ambience of a larger operator, may be an option within your budget.

Craft breweries are proliferating across North America, and some of them rent facilities for wedding ceremonies and/or receptions. Some charge very low fees because they supply the beverages and sometimes the food for the reception.

1.6 College or university campus

Almost universally, institutions of higher education feature plazas, lawn areas, gazebos, chapels, and other attractive amenities. Some even offer ballrooms suitable for indoor wedding ceremonies. Many of these schools rent space for weddings, at reasonable prices.

1.7 Banquet hall

If you choose to hold your reception in a banquet hall, be sure to consider adding decorative flourishes, such as flowers, candles, greenery, and possibly lighting, to boost the ambiance.

1.8 Ranch

Ranch wedding opportunities vary in price, from reasonable to exorbitant. This type of venue offers a peaceful, old-timey backdrop to a wedding celebration, and usually contains any number of ideal locations for wedding portraits — with livestock and without!

1.9 Small-town charm and price

As mentioned earlier, venues in major metropolitan areas are usually more expensive than the equivalent facilities in a smaller city or town. You can save considerably on venue costs for the ceremony and reception, but note that your vendor selection will be narrower, and if you hire vendors from a larger population center, you'll likely have to pay travel fees.

2. Strategize: The Outdoor Wedding

No doubt about it, outdoor wedding ceremonies and receptions in beautiful spots have great appeal. Many lower-priced venue options such as parks, gardens, beaches, and other public sites are ideal for fresh-air nuptials. In California, for example, San Diego County issues permits to use picnic areas, gazebos, and some facilities with buildings, for prices ranging from about $150 to $650, with an extra $50 fee for any catering. In New York City, couples can marry in Central Park for a $400 permit fee, with a $100 additional fee for photography. At Salt Lake City Park, in Utah, the City charges $161 for a permit to hold a wedding ceremony, and offers pavilions for receptions for less than $50.

You will need to ensure that upon your reservation of an outdoor wedding location, and payment of any deposit or fees, you receive a location booking contract specifying the date, time of use, cost, specific location, and any additional fees including overtime or cleanup costs.

You can hold your wedding on a lawn, in an open field, beside the waves, between beds of roses — but you are at the mercy of the weather. Your need to provide shelter for guests depends on the weather that will occur during your ceremony and reception. Ideally, the venue you arrange for has a covered area large enough to hold the event in case of adverse weather, be it rain or severe heat. That's not always possible, however.

Event tents can be rented to protect wedding participants and guests from weather. When both the ceremony and reception are held at the same outdoor location, the dining tent can stand in as a backup venue for the ceremony, in case of rain, hail, or excessive heat. It may turn out that favorable weather means you don't need the tent, and if you've reserved one, you can cancel the day before but under most rental agreements you'll lose your deposit, usually 50 percent of the rental fee.

For public spaces, you will need to contact the agency responsible for approving location use, and book a location for your wedding and/ or reception. Parks and other public sites fall under various jurisdictions, so if this option interests you, take a look at sites in city, state, provincial, and national parks, or historic areas and locations that are operated at the city, state, provincial, and national levels. Remember that bylaws and laws on use of public areas such as parks, gardens, historic sites, and beaches can vary from town to town, county to county, and state to state.

When making arrangements to book outdoor locations for wedding ceremonies and receptions, find out what permits and fees are required for the events themselves, and for any temporary shelters, amplified music, photography, furniture set up, alcoholic beverage service, and food service. Be sure to bring copies of all required booking contracts, permits, and fee-payment receipts to the site. Contracts with service providers for outdoor weddings must specify that the service provider has responsibility for the cleanup.

Some outdoor venues have indoor facilities as well, that can be booked for wedding ceremonies and receptions, or are included with the outdoor facilities. Some outdoor venues have tables and chairs available for use or for rental. If no furniture is provided, your caterer may be able to provide furniture rental, or you will need to rent it, or bring it in yourself.

Also, you must ensure that bathrooms are available during the entirety of your events. Having two toilets and two sinks per 100 people is considered typical. If the location of your ceremony or reception does not have available bathrooms close by, you'll need to rent portable toilets and sinks. At the high end are bathroom trailers with flushing toilets and hot-water sinks; at the lower end are port-a-potties with hand sanitizer.

Keep in mind that portable sinks can run out of water quickly; make sure someone is assigned to check water levels periodically, and refill them as necessary. The same goes for checking that the toilets have an adequate amount of toilet paper.

For an outdoor wedding, in a park, at a beach, in a public garden, or any other public space, you will need to reserve the area to be used, and likely obtain a permit or permits — many jurisdictions require wedding-specific permits. You will need to arrange for tables, chairs, and any shelter such as tents. By using Checklist 2, you can keep track of your outdoor-wedding arrangements. Here, you will keep track of the cost of your outdoor wedding, required permits you have obtained, and deposits and fees you have paid

3. Destination Weddings

One simple method for keeping wedding costs reduced is to have a destination wedding. Now, this may seem counterintuitive: This type of wedding requires travel and accommodation costs that may be higher than those for a local wedding. But here's the key: Typically, only the closest of friends and family are invited, which keeps the guest list minimal, thus slashing catering and venue costs. And for the bride and groom, a destination wedding combines the wedding with the honeymoon!

Of course, if the destination is Fiji, or Patagonia, the wedding could be very expensive for the couple and guests. But a destination wedding need not take place in an exotic overseas locale; North America offers spectacular options, from Rocky Mountain towns such as Banff in Canada and Boulder, Colorado, to ocean-side locations on Vancouver Island, Canada, Myrtle Beach, South Carolina, to fun and exciting cities such as Las Vegas and Montreal. Depending on the location of the bride and groom, nearby paradises such as Puerto Vallarta, Mexico and Hawaii may provide a taste of the exotic at a reasonable cost.

If you're set on a destination wedding, you'll need to start your planning early, and provide more notice to your guests, so they can schedule time off and book travel arrangements. You should be sending your invitations at least four months before the wedding; six months is better. Remember that your choice of destination may affect which of your invitees can come, due to cost and/or duration of travel.

Outdoor Wedding Checklist

Ceremony

[   ]   Location booking contract:

    [   ]   Deposit paid, and date: _____

    [   ]   Fees paid, and date: _____

[   ]   Any required permit(s) for the event:

    [   ]   _____

    [   ]   _____

    [   ]   _____

[   ]   Rented tables and chairs:

    [   ]   Number and description of tables: _____

    [   ]   Number and description of chairs: _____

    [   ]   Deposit paid, and date: _____

    [   ]   Fees paid, and date: _____

[   ]   Flowers

[   ]   Music

[   ]   Rented toilets and sinks

[   ]   Book tent(s), shelters:

    [   ]   Deposit paid, and date: _____

    [   ]   Fees paid, and date: _____

Reception

[   ]   Location booking contract

    [   ]   Reserve outdoor venue space

    [   ]   Deposit paid, and date: _____

    [   ]   Fees paid, and date: _____

[   ]   Any required permit(s) for the event:

    [   ]   Any required permit(s) for food: _____

    [   ]   Any required permit(s) for alcohol: _____

    [   ]   _____

    [   ]   _____

[   ]   Catering

[   ]   Linens, and/or napkins

[   ]   Flowers

[   ]   Decor

[   ]   Rented toilets and sinks

[   ]   Lighting, decorative and/or functional, if required

[   ]   Rented tables and chairs:

    [   ]   Number and description of tables: _____

    [   ]   Number and description of chairs: _____

    [   ]   Deposit paid, and date: _____

    [   ]   Fees paid, and date: _____

    [   ]   Rented linens, and/or napkins: _____

[   ]   Book tent(s), shelters

    [   ]   Deposit paid, and date: _____

    [   ]   Fees paid, and date: _____

Also, you'll have to start planning far enough in advance to ensure that you can book accommodations, venues, and vendors on your chosen date.

For a destination wedding, as well as a honeymoon, time of year greatly affects cost. High seasons, which usually feature the best weather, are the most expensive. Timing your wedding on a date shortly before or after the high season can reduce expenses, and maximize the chances of excellent weather.

Warning: If you're marrying in a foreign country, some have residency-related requirements mandating that a marriage is only legal if the couple has been in the country for a certain amount of time.

Planning a destination wedding involves another challenge: Obtaining vendors from a distance. If possible, you should make a preliminary planning trip to the destination, to meet and coordinate with vendors, whom you've selected through the process in this book. If such a trip is not possible, it may make sense to hold your event at a resort that offers wedding packages, and will take care of the arrangements. Note that some of your guests may prefer to stay elsewhere, and your resort may charge fees for outside visitors.

Make sure you're at least as diligent in researching vendors, including the venue and accommodation providers, as you would for a local wedding. Get references. Check online review sites. Meet with vendors, or if that's not possible, chat with them via video link so you can make an assessment based on their manner and degree of professionalism. When vendors quote costs, find out what their total cost will be, including taxes and any fees. If you find a vendor you like and trust, you can ask that person to recommend other vendors.

Your guests will be making a substantial commitment in time and money to attend your wedding, and you should help them as much as possible by making arrangements for hotel rooms (ideally at discounted rates), and providing information about transport from the airport to the hotel. When you reserve a block of rooms for your guests, ensure you have it in writing that any rooms not booked by a specific time will be taken out of the reservation; otherwise, you may be on the hook for the cost of the whole block, occupied or not. If you're having your wedding at a resort, when you're negotiating a package cost for specific goods and services, use the fact that you're bringing guests to their resort as a negotiating point: You should be able to gain price concessions based on the business you're bringing to them.

It's typical with destination weddings to show gratitude to the guests by providing welcome bags or baskets containing goodies useful at the destination (e.g., champagne in Las Vegas, or disposable underwater cameras in Maui) as well as local maps and attraction lists. For single guests, you can express your gratitude further by linking them with other single people of the same gender to share a room, if they wish.

Often, couples will pay for one event during the wedding trip that the guests and wedding party enjoy together. This may be a welcome dinner, or an adventure trip such as kayaking or snorkeling, or a sunset cruise.

If you're planning a wedding in a foreign country, be aware that currency exchange rates can affect prices, and can change significantly, either raising or lowering expenses.

Some couples rely on local vendors but bite the bullet to bring in their own photographer. This will add to the cost of the wedding, but provide some security that the wedding photos will be satisfactory. However, some foreign countries will require noncitizens, including wedding photographers and other vendors, to have permits to work.

A word to brides concerning dresses: Travel can wrinkle clothes! No matter how well you pack your dress, chances are it will need steaming, so make sure you can have that done as soon as possible after your arrival at the destination.

4. Visualize: What You Need to Know before Contacting Venues

By using Worksheet 5 (Top 5 Vendor Choices), from Chapter 3, you will know who you want to contact about venues. Once you have decided the date of your wedding, your first question should be whether or not the venue is available for your special day. This way you can rule out a venue quickly if it's unavailable.

Before you call, gather the following information because the representative of the venue will need to know the answers:

- Date (and day of week) of ceremony and/or reception.
- Start time of ceremony and/or reception.
- Finish time of ceremony and/or reception.
- Whether or not you want the venue to cater the reception.
- Expected number of guests.
- Tableware specifications.
- Table linens and napkins specifications.
- Additional tables required for cocktail reception, cake, and guest book.

Checklist 3 provides you with a list of questions to ask the venue representative. By printing the checklist from the download kit, you can make notes as you are talking to the person.

When you are considering booking a venue, arrange to meet the venue representative at the venue. Look closely at the facilities to be used for the event, including the kitchen. Ask further questions or follow up on questions you asked during your initial phone call. Ask to see the venue's standard contract and read it carefully. If discussions produce satisfactory results, obtain a contract from the venue. Once you are satisfied that all your needs will be met, sign and return the venue contract with the deposit immediately, or by the specified date. Remember to contact the venue one month in advance of the wedding to confirm details of timing and services.

[   ]   Are you available on our wedding date?

[   ]   Do you have the facilities to accommodate our needs, including guest numbers?

[   ]   What is the price for the venue space?

[   ]   What is the amount of deposit and due date?

[   ]   What are the off-peak rates?

[   ]   Do you allow in-house catering only?

[   ]   Is there a fee for outside catering?

[   ]   Is there a fees for music performance?

[   ]   Do you allow in-house bar service only?

[   ]   What is the fee to bring in a cake from an outside source?

[   ]   What is the fee for outside bar service or customer-provided alcohol?

[   ]   Are permits/licenses required for food and/or alcoholic beverage service?

[   ]   Can you provide parking for set up by the florist, caterer, music provider(s), and photographer?

[   ]   Are there cleanup fees?

[   ]   Are there security fees?

[   ]   Do you require a damage deposit?

[   ]   What is the opening time and the amount of time allotted to set up?

[   ]   What is the closing time?

If the meeting doesn't result in an agreement to proceed, move on to the next venue in your Top 5 list.

5. Scrutinize: Understanding the Venue Contract

The following points show you what topics should be covered in your venue contract:

- **Cancellation policy:** You will pay a penalty if you cancel the event. The penalty amount is based on the timing of cancellation. Because venue managers have a harder time rebooking an event when the cancellation is made at short notice, penalties are ordinarily higher the closer to the event date that the cancellation occurs. Typically the highest penalty is levied for canceling less than a month from the event date. Another penalty amount may cover cancellation between one and six months before the event date. The lowest penalty amount is likely to be imposed for a cancellation more than six months before the event date.

- **Estimated guest count:** Payment to the venue is based on the estimated guest count, and is typically final — should the number of guests turn out to be fewer than the estimate, the cost will be the same, but some venues may provide additional services, such as menu additions, to keep the cost consistent with the services and goods provided.

- **Final guest count:** Typically must be provided to the venue no later than three working days before the event.

- **Food and beverages:** Unless the contract specifies that the client may bring specified foods and beverages to the venue, all outside food and beverages are typically prohibited.

- **Alcohol:** If it is "per-drink charging," the client pays the venue according to how much consumption of alcoholic beverages occurs, which is based on the number of bottles of alcoholic beverages that are consumed. The venue will have a formula to determine the number of drinks.

  If it is "per-person, per-hour charging," the client pays the venue based on the number of guests and the number of hours during which beverages are served.

- **Payment:** Full payment is typically due 10 business days before the event. A final estimate of expenses will likely include an "overage" charge, often 20 percent, to cover any potential changes once payment has been made. All or part of the overage fee will be returned if there no additional costs, or if the additional costs do not amount to the total overage fee.

- **Service fees:** Many venues will add mandatory service fees to all food and beverage services.

- **Cleanup fee:** Some venues impose an automatic cleanup fee.

- **Overtime fee:** Most venues impose a charge for events that go past the closing time specified in the contract.

- **Insurance fees:** Some venues impose insurance fees.

- **Damage fees:** Some venues require damage deposits or impose specified damage fees.

Checklist 4 will help you itemize what details should be included in your venue contract.

[ ] Client name.

[ ] Date (and day of week) of wedding and/or reception.

[ ] Phone number for client.

[ ] Name and cell phone number of alternate person the venue provider can call on the wedding day in the event of an issue.

[ ] Location of venue.

[ ] Location of wedding site.

[ ] Location of reception site.

[ ] Total cost, including taxes and fees.

[ ] Amount of deposit (based on approximate guest count).

[ ] Estimated guest count.

[ ] Final guest count.

[ ] Closing time.

[ ] Fee to bring in cake from an outside source.

[ ] Performed music fees.

[ ] Cleanup fees.

[ ] Overtime fees.

[ ] Insurance fees.

[ ] Damage deposit/fees.

[ ] Permits and licenses, if any (e.g., health/food service; liquor).

[ ] Must specify permitted arrival/set-up times for vendors:

    [ ] Caterer.

    [ ] Photographer.

    [ ] Florist.

    [ ] Music provider.

    [ ] Cake delivery.

    [ ] Items to be delivered to site before wedding day.

5

Finding the Caterer and the Wedding Cake

Wanting more than they can afford is the most common mistake couples make with regard to catering. Let's be honest: If you hire a chef from a Michelin-star restaurant to cater your wedding reception, your guests will remember the meal. However, let's be honest again: For nearly every kind of meal served at a wedding reception, memories of the food will be far down the list of recollections for you and your guests. And that's fine.

You want food that will taste good, and be provided in sufficient quantity. You don't have to serve a fancy meal. Opportunities abound for creative, reasonably priced options.

Before you start shopping for a caterer, note that if you haven't decided on a venue, it could turn out that your eventual choice of venue may have its own food service, and will not allow you to use an outside caterer.

1. Visualize: Your Reception

Your vision of the reception should cover the kinds of food to be served, and how that food will be served. Here are some questions to consider:

- What types of food service are most important for your wedding reception?

- Do you want to serve impressive appetizers, and put less emphasis on the meal (or perhaps the other way around)?

- Is a dinner reception crucial, or could you arrange your wedding day schedule so you are married in the morning and have a reception brunch, which would be less expensive?

- Could you skip a sit-down meal and turn your reception into a cocktails-and-snacks event?

- Do you require a formal, sit-down dinner in which servers deliver multiple courses, or would serve-yourself stations work?

1.1 Strategize: Catering options

In large cities, catering prices generally rise. By taking a little initiative and you can find options that will reduce expenses, and ensure you and your guests are very happy with the food and beverages.

Many caterers offer various packages, each including different types of food service, and usually priced per-person, whether it's for plated meals, buffets, family meals, or hors d'oeuvres selection. One strategy is to simply pick a package that suits your budget. Ask the caterer for a detailed price list covering all menu items so you have as much information as possible and can create your menu using appealing dishes that aren't high priced because they're out of season or trendy.

Important Note: Brides and grooms, don't forget to include yourselves, and wedding party members, when providing the caterer with a guest count!

Consider the following options:

- Catered meals generally start at around $15 per person for buffet or family style service, not including bar costs, and can climb steeply from there. Buffets and family style meals have an added benefit of encouraging guests to socialize, and can make the meal more fun. Buffets also allow for easy accommodation of various food preferences.

- Plated dinners start at around $20 per person, and often there are additional charges for serving staff, which can be $25 per hour and up, and for tableware, glassware, and cutlery rentals, plus furniture rentals, if required.

- If your venue does not include tables and chairs, or tableware, glassware, cutlery, and linens, and your caterer does not include them in the food prices, rental costs can add to the previous prices listed — often $15 to $25 per person — although some caterers include those goods in the per-person price.

- For a plated dinner and full bar, per-person costs can easily top $75; although, they may be lower if the venue provides the catering and includes tableware, glassware, cutlery, and linens.

- Depending on the caterer, and the menu, a buffet can cost less than a plated, three- or four-course meal.

- Mix camaraderie with economy by serving family style shared platters at each table. This type of service is usually considerably less expensive than a plated meal due to lower food preparation costs and reduced need for serving staff. But make sure your tables are big enough to accommodate the platters and allow them to be passed around easily — having smaller centerpieces helps.

- Instead of serving chicken breasts, serve a pasta dish featuring chicken, which is less expensive than a chicken breast entrée.

- Beef is often a more expensive entrée item than chicken, pork, or some fish.

- Provide fun, serve-yourself dishes such as a fajitas and taco bar, a Thai or Chinese food bar, or a pasta bar. This will cost much less than a multi-course formal dinner.

- Consider scheduling your ceremony and reception so you have an afternoon meal with a picnic lunch theme such as salads, fried chicken, and fancy cookies.

- Consider scheduling your ceremony and reception so you have a brunch reception, serving fruit, quiche or frittatas, bagels and smoked salmon, coffee, tea, beer, wine, and sparkling wine or mimosas.

- Stick with foods that are in season as an effective strategy for keeping your expenses as low as possible.

- Keep entrée selections to one or two options (with accommodation for guests with dietary restrictions) can help you stay within your budget.

- Hors d'oeuvres can cost almost as much as a plated dinner, especially if you require servers to pass them around. Putting trays on tables can cost less, but guests tend to eat more than if items are passed around by servers. However, having a few appetizer stations, with items set out in relatively small batches and replenished when depleted can encourage guests to engage with each other, and add to their enjoyment, while limiting food expense and waste.

- Simple, plain white tableware and clear glassware always look good for a wedding reception, and are usually less expensive choices.

- If you've chosen a fairly informal meal, consider compostable tableware and cutlery; it can be significantly less expensive than rented items. You may want to stick with glass for any bar and wine service.

- Use mid-range liquor brands instead of top-shelf brands to reduce bar costs.

- Reduce dessert costs by offering individualized delicacies such as cake pops, mini-cheesecakes, tarts, cupcakes, chocolate-covered strawberries, and macaroons.

- Eliminate additional dessert costs by serving only wedding cake for dessert.

- For refreshments, you don't need to replicate a bar: You can keep guests happy with beer, wine, and one or two signature cocktails, perhaps favorites of the bride and groom. Keeping beverage selection simple can also mean fewer bartenders, for additional savings.

For every element of the food and beverage service, you can make choices that will reduce costs. Of course, your best way to reduce catering costs is to keep guest numbers as low as possible. As for what you will serve, if it's a formal dinner, the meat doesn't have to be filet mignon; braised short ribs, for instance, are a tasty and much less expensive meat dish. Serving crème brûlée to each guest will cost a lot;

however, allowing them to choose their own mini-desserts won't set you back nearly as much, and your guests will enjoy them.

Important: Be mindful that most caterers impose overtime charges if your event runs past the scheduled end, especially if catering staff must stay longer.

Restaurants that host wedding receptions, depending on the menu prices, can be a less-expensive option than hiring a venue and caterer separately, as you eliminate delivery charges and possibly all or most rental charges for tableware, glassware, cutlery, linens, and furniture. Quite possibly, one of your favorite restaurants does catering. If you find the idea of serving food you know and love, check around with some of your favorite moderately priced restaurants, and see if they can cater your reception.

If you are hosting the reception in someone's home or a very small venue, you could arrange (well in advance) delivery of food from your favorite restaurant.

Some colleges and universities have competitively priced catering services, and cater on- and off-site. Many culinary institutes (e.g., "chef schools") offer catering, which can be more economical than hiring a professional caterer company, particularly if the meals are prepared by student chefs, under the supervision of an instructor chef.

1.1a Strategize: Do-It-Yourself Catering

If you're having your reception in a private home, or a venue that allows food and drink to be brought in from outside, you have options for greatly reducing your food and beverage costs by supplying them yourself. You may also avoid renting tableware, linens, glasses, and cutlery by using disposable products (many such products are made from recycled products or are recyclable). Also, remember that some venues require permits for food and alcoholic beverage service.

Depending on the size of your wedding, and your budget, and the availability of great cooks among your family and friends, you could serve home-cooked food, and beverages you've bought in bulk (e.g., beer on tap and reasonably priced wine).

One option can save a great deal of money: The potluck meal, in which guests bring home-cooked dishes for your reception. You'll need to cover appetizers, salads, vegetables, entrées, and desserts. You can ask each guest or couple to make a dish to serve a designated number of people, but you don't want to put a huge burden on them, so ask them to make enough to serve 10 people. Then delegate the dish production to enough guests or couples so that each making ten servings will add up to the total number of attendees. Be mindful that guests may feel left out if you haven't asked them to contribute anything, so make the request to everyone. You'll have to make sure that your venue allows outside food (you may have to negotiate this when you're booking the venue), and that you have access to refrigeration and food-heating facilities, if necessary.

Tip: Don't ask guests to bring soup to a potluck meal because you'll have to provide bowls, while otherwise you can keep tableware to plates and cutlery.

1.2 Minimize: Bar costs

Alcoholic beverage charges are usually based on either a per-drink or per-person cost. Which arrangement makes sense for you largely depends on how much alcohol you expect your guests to drink. When you're arranging for bar service, make sure your expected guest number accounts for the anticipated numbers of minors and other non-drinkers. Bar budgets are usually calculated on the basis of one alcohol-drinking guest consuming one drink per hour that the bar is open.

With per-drink charging, the client pays the caterer according to how much consumption of alcoholic beverages occurs, which is based on the number of bottles of alcoholic beverages that are consumed. The venue will have a formula to determine the number of drinks from the number of bottles used.

With per-person, per-hour charging, the client pays the venue based on the number of guests and the number of hours during which beverages are served. Per-drink charging can make sense when guests don't drink a lot, but if they do, your bar tab can increase quickly!

To save money on bar costs, serve beer, wine, and one or two signature cocktails. Also, close the bar during dinner, and an hour before the end of the reception.

Skip the champagne toast because it can add hundreds of dollars in costs for champagne and glassware fees. Some couples are very attached to the idea, and should spend the money if it's a priority, but the cost can run from $1.50 per person, based on $5 champagne and basic rented champagne flutes, to $3 per person with $14 champagne and basic crystal flutes, to upwards of $10 per person based on high-end champagne and fancy crystal. If you take the mid-range option, you're still looking at a $300 cost for 100 attendees.

Alcoholic beverages can suck up a massive portion of your budget, especially if you use a catering company that requires that they provide the refreshments. To strike a major blow at beverage costs, pick a caterer who will let you take responsibility for the refreshments. Some caterers will also provide a bartending service using beverages you've purchased. Or hire a bartending service (you need a bonded bartender). In either case, work with the bartending service to determine how much of each type of beverage needs to be on hand, buy it yourself at a liquor discounter, and you'll have saved a pile of money. Coordinate with the venue to determine if it has a liquor license, and if not, whether the venue will obtain a liquor permit for your event or whether that will be your responsibility.

1.3 Visualize: What you need to know before contacting caterers

By using Worksheet 5 (Top 5 Vendor Choices), from Chapter 3, you will know who you want to contact about catering. Once you have decided the date of your reception, your first question should be whether or not the catering company is available for that day. This way you can rule out a company quickly if it's unavailable.

Before you call, gather the following information because the caterer will need to know the answers:

- Date (and day of week) of the reception.

- Start time of the reception.

- Food service timing.

- Location.

- Expected number of guests.

- Type of food service (i.e., brunch, lunch, cocktail reception, supper).

- Manner of food service (e.g., formal sit-down meal, buffet, tapas stations, barbecue, hors d'oeuvres).

- Refreshments to be served by caterer, if any, including alcoholic and nonalcoholic beverages.

- Expected number of vegetarian, vegan, and/or dietary restricted guests.

- Dress preference for serving staff.

- Furniture required, if caterer is to provide.

- Tableware preferences, if caterer is to provide.

- Linen and napkin preferences, if caterer is to provide.

- Whether you will have other vendors, such as a photographer and music providers on site during the reception who will require meals. Note that some caterers charge for these meals, and some do not. If you will be requiring meals for vendors, attempt to negotiate away this cost.

- Your catering budget. Reputable caterers have specific prices for specific goods and services, so they need to know your budget so they can tell you what they can provide; from that point, there's room for negotiation).

After contacting the caterers in your Top 5 list, and asking them the questions in Checklist 5, arrange for a tasting session with your first choice. (**Note:** It can cost hundreds of dollars in labor, food, equipment, and linens for a caterer to provide a tasting session. If you like the food, you will need to confirm the caterer's availability for the reception date and obtain a copy of the contract. Remember to contact the caterer at least one month in advance of the wedding to confirm details of timing and services.

If the meeting doesn't result in an agreement to proceed, move on to the next caterer in your Top 5 list.

1.4 Scrutinize: Understanding the catering contract

As with other vendors, you need to have a detailed contract with the caterer that spells out exactly what food and services the caterer will provide. The caterer's standard contract may not have space to detail all goods and services, so additional pages may be required. Checklist 6 shows you what your catering contract must contain so you can feel confident that all will go smoothly on your wedding day.

What You Need to Ask the Caterer

[   ]   Are you available on the wedding reception date?

[   ]   Level of experience with wedding receptions: How long have you been in business? How many weddings do you do per year?

[   ]   Can you provide three references? (If so, contact them and ask them about the positives and negatives of working with that caterer.)

[   ]   Are you licensed for food service in the jurisdiction where the reception will be held?

[   ]   Does you have liability insurance?

[   ]   What options are available for meals?

[   ]   Can you provide a detailed price list of all menu items?

[   ]   Can you provide vegetarian, vegan, halal, kosher meals, and/ or dietary restrictions if guest list requires it?

[   ]   Is there a special rate for children 12 and younger such as free or discounted meals? (If you will have a lot of children at your reception, attempt to secure free meals for them.)

[   ]   What decor is provided for food tables?

[   ]   What are the fees for buffet and sit-down meals?

[   ]   What are the fees for served appetizers versus appetizer table?

[   ]   What are the fees for serve-yourself food stations?

[   ]   What are the per-person costs for meals?

[   ]   What are the fees for food-service equipment such as serving trays and chafing dishes?

[   ]   Will other vendors attending, such as photographers and musicians, be provided with meals or will it cost per person?

[   ]   What are the cake-cutting and cake-serving fees, if any? (Attempt to negotiate away these fees, if applicable.)

[   ]   How many bartenders will be provided? (One bartender for every 50 to 70 people is ideal. Any more than 100 people per bartender usually leads to long lines.)

[   ]   Do you allow clients to bring their own alcohol (corkage fee may apply)?

[   ]   What are the style of dress options for attending managers and workers?

[   ]   Will permits be required for serving food and alcohol at the venue selected?

       [   ]   Will the caterer obtain the permits?

       [   ]   Are you licensed to serve alcohol?

[   ]   Will there be an on-site manager or coordinator to oversee preparation and the food and beverage service?

[   ]   Will you provide tables, chairs, and/or linens? (Compare the items and prices to those you could rent yourself.)

[   ]   What is the total amount of tax?

[   ]   Is there a gratuity or service charge? If so, how much?

[   ]   Are you, the caterer, responsible for all cleanup of catering-related services?

       [   ]   Is there a cleanup fee?

[   ]   Is there a delivery fee?

CHECKLIST 6
Catering Contract Details

[ ] Client name.

[ ] Date (and day of week) of the reception.

[ ] Phone number for client.

[ ] To-be spouse's name, email address, and telephone number.

[ ] Name and cell phone number of alternate person the caterer can call on the wedding day in event of an issue.

[ ] Cell phone number of catering representative on wedding day.

[ ] Estimated guest count (including the bride and groom).

    [ ] Final guest count due date.

    [ ] Overage charge for food served beyond the final guest count.

[ ] Location of venue for catering.

[ ] Location of catering location within venue.

[ ] Detailed menu.

[ ] Time(s) of food service.

[ ] Time(s) of beverage service.

[ ] Cost of rental items (negotiate to waive rental fees, if possible):

    [ ] Tableware, glasses, cutlery.

    [ ] Furniture.

    [ ] Linens.

    [ ] Other items.

[ ] Total cost, including taxes and fees.

[ ] Caterer set-up time (coordinate with venue).

[ ] Attire of catering staff.

[ ] Catering service ending time.

[ ] Catering staff fees.

[ ] Fees for food-service equipment such as serving trays and chafing dishes.

[ ] Amount of deposit (based on approximate guest count).

[ ] Delivery fees.

[ ] Cleanup fees.

[ ] Overtime fees.

[ ] Insurance fees.

[ ] Damage deposit/fees.

[ ] Cancellation fee.

[ ] Refund policy.

[ ] Other fees.

[ ] Final payment due date.

2. Visualize: The Wedding Cake

A big, elaborate, multilayer cake can set you back more than $1,000. An artfully decorated smaller cake can make an equally strong impression, at a much lower cost. Your gem of a cake is beautifully symbolic, and here's the trick: If it isn't large enough to serve all your guests, you can buy an accompanying flat cake with frosting that matches or complements the wedding cake, and have it cut in the kitchen, and then served.

Wedding cakes come in a variety of sizes, to suit the number of diners. If you want a traditional, tiered wedding cake, you can find a pretty one for $2 to $5 per diner, and you can buy one in a smaller size that your bakery of choice produces. That bakery will almost certainly sell flat cakes at a per-person cost as low as $1.25.

Keep in mind that typically only 75 to 85 percent of guests have a slice of cake, so decide your cake size accordingly. However, if you have both bride and groom cakes, many guests will have a slice of each. Also, if you're serving a dessert, you can have a smaller wedding cake.

You can reduce costs further if you choose a nontraditional wedding cake. A flat-out gorgeous confection, decorated beautifully, perhaps accessorized with a few flowers, that costs less than a traditional cake because you're choosing a smaller size (and because many bakeries charge a premium price for wedding cakes). Consider a variety of small desserts, artfully displayed, next to the smaller cake — lemon bars, macaroons, and cake pops all make fun, elegant statements.

Here's are some ways to keep cake costs reduced:

- Keep it low: The fewer the tiers, the lower the price, in general.

- Stick with butter-cream frosting, rather than more expensive but less tasty fondant.

- Choose standard icing flavors, such as vanilla or lemon.

- For multitiered cakes, keep the same flavor of filling between the tiers.

- Avoid costly fillings such as cream cheese, chocolate, and nut-based fillings.

- Stick with standard filling flavors such as almond cream, vanilla cream, pineapple cream, and preserves-and-cream, rather than fillings containing fresh fruit.

- Keep the cake's decorations simple — elaborate frostings and decorations can increase the price considerably. Icing dots or "pearls" can provide a lovely touch for a relatively minimal cost, as can a few small flowers. If you plan to harmonize the cake colors with your wedding palette (recommended!), provide color swatches to the baker.

- Buy a cake from a licensed home baker, if available in your jurisdiction. A home baker's prices are often lower than those at bakeries.

- You can eliminate cake delivery charges by picking up the cake, or assigning the task to a helper; as you can imagine, this choice carries risk! A cake may need refrigeration during transport, which will probably be difficult for you to provide. Of course, accidents happen — either on the road (even a mild fender bender could be disastrous for the cake) or while the cake is being carried.

- Because the cake cutting is often a memorable and symbolic event, many couples elect to buy their own cake knife, to keep afterward as a memento. Most bakers and caterers can provide rented cake knives for couples who don't wish to purchase their own.

Here are some other tips to make sure your day goes smoothly:

- Your cake will probably be delivered hours before the reception. Consult with the baker about refrigeration requirements, and if refrigeration is necessary, ensure you'll have access to refrigeration facilities at the reception venue.

- Ensure you've arranged for a cake table, and make sure it's level before the cake is placed on it!

- Don't place the cake in direct, hot sunlight or a hot area while it's on display.

- If your reception will be held in a location and time of year of significant heat, you'll need to make sure the baker creates a cake that won't melt. Buttercream is particularly vulnerable to melting, and can do so if sitting in direct sunlight. Fondant is more expensive, but more stable; however, high heat can even melt fondant. Your baker may have tricks to reduce the possibility of melting. In any case, if the area where the cake is to be displayed will be hot, you'll have to keep the cake refrigerated until it's brought out, and minimize the amount of time the cake is out before it's cut and served.

- Be aware that nearly all bakeries produce goods containing milk, wheat, nuts, and other allergens, and that even if your cake is free of such items, guests with severe allergies may be vulnerable.

2.1 Wedding cake contract

With the cake baker, you will be entering into a contractual arrangement. Checklist 7 shows you what the wedding cake contract should contain.

CHECKLIST 7
Wedding Cake Contract Details

[ ] Wedding date, and day of week.

[ ] Number of guests.

[ ] Reception location.

[ ] Name, email address, and cell phone number for wedding day contact person.

[ ] Names, cell phone numbers, and email addresses of bride and groom.

[ ] Name and cell phone number of florist (if there will be floral decoration on or around the cake).

    [ ] Time of flower delivery (if there will be floral decoration on or around the cake).

    [ ] Description of flower arrangement on or around cake (if there will be floral decoration on or around the cake).

[ ] Style and description of cake: Number of layers, colors, type of border, and number of tiers; shape: round, square, or rectangular.

    [ ] Cake flavor.

    [ ] Icing selection.

    [ ] Filling selection.

    [ ] Description of cake decorations.

    [ ] Exact wording of writing to be on cake, if any.

    [ ] Cake size.

[ ] Cake price.

[ ] Date cake will be baked (it should be baked the day before the wedding).

[ ] Supplemental sheet cake, including, price, size, and description, if applicable.

[ ] Cake stand, cake knife, cake plates (if not provided by the caterer or venue), and cake server rental prices, if any (if the baker charges for these items, try to negotiate to eliminate the charge).

    [ ] Deposit amounts for cake stand, cake knife, cake plates, and cake server.

    [ ] Date rental items must be returned to the bakery.

[ ] Cake delivery time.

    [ ] Delivery method (a refrigerated vehicle or vehicle with a refrigerated area may be necessary depending on the distance between the bakery and the reception, and the weather).

[ ] Delivery charge (including any extra fee if the cake is to be delivered on a day the bakery is closed, including holidays).

[ ] Flower placement charge (if you choose to have floral decoration on or around the cake, try to negotiate with the baker to provide flower placement at no charge).

[ ] Cancellation policy, with timeline describing penalties for client cancellation.

[ ] Specified backup baker, such as an assistant, who will create the cake if the designated baker is unavailable for reasons such as illness, family emergency, or accident.

6

Choosing a Photographer

For many couples and their families, the photography is a key element of the vendor list. The images the photographer captures will be treasured for the entire lives of the bride and groom and their friends and loved ones.

The wedding is your story of love and friendship, of two lives coming together, and of two families coming together. So it's very important to choose a photographer who can provide the images that will tell your story, a story that you and your loved ones and friends will revisit in the years to come.

It's a fact that just about anybody can take snapshots. However, producing high-quality images that capture the beauty and emotion of an event, that tell stories of love and friendship, is a task for a professional. Your photographer needs to have technical skill, plus an eye for beauty and for capturing the critical moments that make up an event. He or she also must be intimately familiar, through experience, with weddings — to know when those important emotional moments will occur; to know where to take up the best position in order to get that perfect, beautiful shot at the exact perfect time; to know how to make a wedding couple and the wedding party feel comfortable and relaxed so the photos represent the interplay of personalities and people that make the best wedding images sing with beauty and joy that will spill forth from the pictures forever. And your photographer must be organized, and business-wise, so the shooting goes smoothly, and you receive the service and images you've paid for, on time and without hassles and delays.

Professional photographers are expensive. You'll be hard put to find one who will charge less than $600 for a few hours of wedding photography, which can cover some preparation, the ceremony, some portraits, and the beginning of the reception. The dollar amounts can seem very high if you consider the price per hour, but the photographer also spends a great deal of time processing photos to make them ready for the client.

If your budget is extremely limited, you can consider hiring a student photographer, or finding a professional who will work for a very short period, perhaps only long enough to photograph the ceremony and do a few portraits. Most photographers will be reluctant to book, for example, a two-hour wedding shoot, because they won't want to miss the opportunity, with another client, to book a full day or half day. Scheduling your wedding on an off-peak day of the week, or in the off-season, or even at off-peak hours such as the morning, will increase your chances of finding a photographer willing to sign a contract for a very short wedding shoot.

If your photography plans involve a session between the ceremony and reception, make sure there are snacks available for the bride and groom, and anyone else taking part, including the wedding party. Everyone should be happy in the photos, and preventing hunger pangs helps!

Planning an economical wedding usually means doing without a videographer, which is not a major loss, as most wedding videos are watched seldom or not at all. If you're set on hiring a videographer, you can manage it if you're able to cut costs in other areas.

In general, photography is an area where it is particularly easy to reduce costs without reducing the quality of the photographs.

1. Strategize: Let There Be (Good) Light!

The time of day at which photos are taken has a powerful effect on the quality of the images. In the middle of the day, when the sun is overhead and bright, it casts unsightly shadows onto people's faces, particularly over the eyes. When the light is very bright, it makes for dark shadows, and faces and figures become a mix of shiny hot spots and gloomy dark shapes. Flash photography can reduce the problem, but creates an artificial look that is, for good reason, going out of style.

With today's cameras, skilled photographers can usually compensate for lighting issues without using a flash. The best photos are taken in the morning and afternoon, when sunlight comes in at a slant, softly lighting figures, faces, and backgrounds, without creating dark shadows. Keep this important reality in mind when you're planning when your ceremony will take place, and when the photographer will take portrait photos. If you're planning an outdoor portrait session, make provisions for weather and have a sheltered or indoor backup location or locations in mind. If a backup location is indoors, check to see if any fees are required for photography.

2. Visualize: Look into the Future

Look into the future. Where, exactly, do you want the images from your wedding to live on? Most likely, you want them to live in frames on the walls of your home, and in the homes of your close family members. You probably want them to live on in a wedding scrapbook. In this day and age, you almost certainly want to collect them electronically, stored on computers, filed away on hard drives and memory sticks, possibly even organized into an electronic scrapbook.

Who should be in these photos that will hang on walls, look out from a scrapbook, and fly around the world via email and social media? For most people, the important photos are portraits of the bride and groom, portraits of the couple with the wedding party, and a portrait of the two with all the family members who attend the wedding. But don't neglect to ensure your photographer will take candids along the way, to catch moments from your wedding you'll want to keep in an album and share on social media.

2.1 Prioritize: Choose your shots

With an unlimited budget, you could have a dozen photographers documenting every nanosecond of your wedding day, from the moment you awake until you leave the reception together to start your new life. But you want to keep costs reasonable. With photography, you have simple methods for keeping down expenditures.

In this step, you choose what parts of the wedding day are most important to memorialize in photographs so think about what you've visualized. Twenty-five years from now, what sort of photos do you want to still be sharing on social media, and viewing in your wedding album, or have hanging on your wall, or on your parents' walls? What images will you want to look at over and over, for as long as you live? The answers to these questions form your "shot list" — the elements of the wedding, and the specific scenes your photographer must shoot. Because you're not going to have every nanosecond of the wedding documented photographically, you're going to plan for the shots that represent the essence of your wedding. Photos of the ceremony, and portraits of the bride and groom — alone and with family and wedding party members — are usually the images brides and grooms treasure the most. At the ceremony, key photographic moments include the following:

- The bride and groom catching sight of each other for the first time. (There may be tears!)

- The parents of the bride and groom giving them away.

- Glances between the couple.

- The ring exchange.

- The kiss. Here's a tip: The longer the kiss, the better chance the photographer will get a great photo!

- Photos of the just-married couple walking together up the aisle capture another cherished ceremony moment.

- For portraits, it's important to make sure to focus on photos of the bride and groom with close family members, as well as on the couple with the wedding party — the family pictures hold deep meaning for couples, and their families, in the years to come.

Chances are, photos of the bride with her hair in curlers or only half her makeup done will not make the list of most-cherished photos, so consider cutting out the "getting ready" shots.

Whatever the scene, event, or location, the photos that make the strongest impressions, and are treasured and shared the most, are those that convey the emotion of the day, that capture the feelings behind the special moments.

3. Strategize: A Service to Suit Your Needs

Wedding photography, of course, is a business, and ultimately the name of the game is profit; a photographer must make a living. However, you'll find great variation in the way photographers earn their money. Some focus on providing expensive scrapbooks; while others focus on charging clients for printed, and sometimes framed, images. These are not the photographers you want. You want a photographer who will provide photography services — not scrapbooking, not photo printing, not framing. You want a photographer — and there are many of these — who will charge you a set price for his or her time, and provide you with a set number of full-resolution, enlargement-ready images that cover your shot list, and which you can use as you wish — for enlargements you will put into frames, for the scrapbook you will create, for emailing, and for posting on social media.

3.1 Scrutinize: Assessing a photographer

These are the three things you need to find out about a photographer:

1. Does he or she make great wedding photos?

2. Does the photographer make you feel comfortable?

3. Does the person conduct himself or herself professionally in every way?

To answer question number 1, you need to see the photographer's work. Any photographer worth his or her salt will have a website, which can give you an idea of what he or she is capable of — at his or her very best. What ends up on the photographer's site will be the cream of the crop. A photographer may have a handful of beautiful photos from a handful of weddings, but that won't necessarily show you how well he or she shoots an entire wedding. Use photographers' websites to help you narrow down your "possibilities" list. When you've narrowed down your list to the Top 3, you need to start looking at more comprehensive portfolios.

For example, you may like your first choice of photographer. You like this person's images. You've seen an artfully posed bride and groom, you've seen a family portrait, and you've seen a fun shot of the couple feeding each other wedding cake. But can this photographer get the key images of all the important elements of your wedding? To determine this, you need to see the whole picture. Ask the photographer to give you access to three weddings he or she has shot — you want to see all the images that were provided to the clients for each wedding. Ask yourself the following questions as you go through the photos:

- Did the photographer take beautiful photos?

- Did the people in the photos look comfortable and natural?

- Did the photographer capture the essential moments of the ceremony?

Another aspect to consider is the mood and emotion you want your wedding photos to reflect; you want to find a photographer whose work reflects that mood. Some couples want their photos to reflect mostly fun; some want them to reflect romance; some want them serious, or conveying religious solemnity. When you're looking at a photographer's portfolio, pay attention to the emotions and moods the photographs showcase, and find a photographer who can capture what you're looking for. Take note of the photographer who shoots candids nice enough to end up in his or her portfolios, which is a good indication of the person's skill; you'll want the photographer you hire to capture some of those moments.

If you're satisfied with the sample imagery the photographer has provided, you need to find out whether that work came easily and naturally, or whether the photographer was a pain-in-the-neck prima donna who obtained excellent photos by bossing everyone around and commandeering the entire wedding event. This is where you need to check references. You should do this in two ways:

- The traditional fashion, by asking for the contact information of several clients whom you've selected from the photographer's portfolio of weddings (mind that the photographer, if he or she chooses the references, is likely to put you in touch only with people she or he knows will say good things).

- Via the Internet, by checking review websites.

When you meet with your photographer, you can find out the answer to question number 2, whether he or she makes you feel comfortable. You want someone skilled, and reliable, but you also want someone fun. Nobody wants a wedding photographer who's all business and no warmth. You want to be having a good time in your portrait sessions, and you want the photos to show it.

Your conversations with a photographer's references, and your examination of online reviews, will provide you with the answer to question number 3 — professional conduct. Find out how the photographer behaved during negotiations over contracts, and throughout wedding shoots. Was the photographer friendly? Did he or she make everyone photographed feel comfortable? Did the person return calls and messages promptly? Did he or she listen to clients and offer creative suggestions for the photography? Did the photographer accomplish what the clients wanted? Most importantly, did the photographer provide the agreed-on photos by the agreed-on time?

3.2 Minimize: Getting the job done

You don't need two photographers. You also don't even need one photographer to work for you the entire wedding day. You need a photographer who will shoot your wedding ceremony, portraits of the bride and groom, wedding party, and the attending family members. This will not take all day so you won't have to pay the full-day price for a photographer.

Some photographers only offer full-day service. Many offer customized options for shorter periods of time, such as four- and six-hour service. If your wedding and reception take place in the morning, you may find a photographer who will offer a two-and-a-half- or three-hour package for a relatively low price, because the early job would allow him or her to book another client for a later event.

Once you've told the photographer what your requirements are, he or she can tell you how much it will cost to perform the required services. If you find the price too high, and cannot agree with the photographer how to reduce the price by adjusting your requirements, move on to the next photographer on your list. If this price is satisfactory, you can continue to the next step, and take a closer look at the photographer's work and client history.

3.3 Strategize: The student photographer

As with your music provider, you can save a lot of money by hiring a student photographer. Remember, the photographer is in charge of creating photos you want to keep forever, and the quality has to be sufficiently good to hang in a frame on your wall, and to give to family and friends.

There are many talented photographers who are still working on their photography education. Some will even work in exchange for transportation costs and meals, with no additional fees. Check with a college or university photography department, or a photography school, or an art academy, to see if they can direct you to students who do freelance wedding photography. Make sure you take a good look at their portfolios, to see the quality of the photos they produce, and get an idea of what sorts of photography they do best. Be advised that some excellent student photographers are accustomed to taking their time setting up every photo you see in their portfolio, and may not perform as well when photographing a dynamic event such as a wedding.

Beware of inexperienced wedding photographers using film cameras instead of digital. Although some highly skilled wedding photographers use film, for an inexperienced photographer it increases the chance that something catastrophic will go wrong. Also, some very artistic student photographers have not yet learned how to take portraits that appear natural and lively. Look for a student who has photographed weddings before, and has photos to show how well he or she did. Also, ensure that the student has backup equipment — at least one extra camera body and lens — in case of a malfunction that could prevent the person from photographing the wedding or completing the job.

3.4 Strategize: Your wedding album

You can pay a photographer hundreds of dollars, or even more than $1,000, to include an album in your photo contract. Or you can create one yourself, using photos the photographer has taken, and others your friends and family have taken from throughout your ceremony and reception.

Ask friends and family to take pictures of any events for which you haven't booked the photographer, such as wedding day preparation, the trip to the ceremony location, candids from the portrait shoot, cutting of the cake, and the socializing and dancing at your reception. These days, even most smartphones can produce good-quality images.

Also, take pictures of items you would typically include in a conventional scrapbook, such as wedding invitations, reception escort cards, and your ceremony program, so you can add them to the photos.

If you would rather have a conventional scrapbook, you can get photos printed at a drug store, and buy a book there, or buy the book at a specialty scrapbooking store, or online. Remember to save artifacts from your wedding day, such as wedding invitations, place cards, ceremony program, and dried flowers.

4. Visualize: What You Need to Know before Contacting Photographers

By using Worksheet 5 (Top 5 Vendor Choices), from Chapter 3, you will know who you want to contact about photography. Once you have decided the date of your wedding, your first question should be whether or not the photographer is available for your special day. This way you can rule out a photographer quickly if he or she is unavailable.

Before you call, gather the following information because the photographer will need to know your answers:

- Date (and day of week) of ceremony and/or reception.
- Ceremony and reception location.
- Ceremony and reception time.
- Portraits location.
- Bridal party means of transportation to and from portrait location.
- Portrait scheduling: Before or during reception.
- Photography budget.
- Wedding events to be photographed:
  - Bride and bridal party preparation.
  - Groom and groomsmen's preparation.
  - Ceremony.
  - Portraits.
- Reception events to be photographed:
  - Set-up of room.
  - Cake cutting.
  - Bouquet toss.
  - First dances.
  - Guest dances.
  - Event candids of bride, groom, and guests.

What You Need to Ask the Photographer

[   ]   Will you be available on our wedding date?

[   ]   How many weddings have you photographed?

[   ]   Do you have backup equipment in case of a malfunction or an accident? (If the answer is "none," that's a big risk.)

[   ]   Do you have three references that I can contact? (You will want to ask the references for their positive and negatives about that photographer.)

[   ]   Do you use film or digital?

[   ]   Can you provide the photographs I require for a price within my budget?

[   ]   Do you provide full-resolution images for my unrestricted use?

[   ]   Do you charge a travel fee?

[   ]   Can I see a portfolio of photos showing a complete ceremony and reception?

[   ]   How long after the wedding will I need to wait to see the photos?

[   ]   Do you have a qualified assistant who will take over the wedding-day photography if you become unavailable due to illness, family emergency, or accident?

After asking the photographer about the questions in Checklist 8, you will next need to ask your first-choice photographer to provide you with all the shots provided for three weddings, so you can evaluate his or her ability to produce great work for an entire wedding event. If the work looks good, continue; if not, go to your next choice on your Top 5 list.

Your next step is to meet with the photographer and, if your in-person meeting satisfies all your concerns, ask to see the standard contract to hammer out the details. Remember to contact the photographer one month in advance of wedding to confirm details of timing and services.

5. Scrutinize: Understanding the Photographer's Contract

As with other vendor contracts, a photographer's standard contract is designed to cover the photographer's bases. You need to make sure everything you've agreed on with the photographer is set out in detail in the contract, from the price, to the number of locations where the photographer will work, to the list of specific shots. Remember that your photographer has much expertise to offer, and listen openly and carefully to suggestions he or she has about tailoring the contract to your needs and budget. Checklist 9 contains everything your contract with the photographer should contain.

Note: It is typical for photographer contracts to include a clause giving them the right to publish your photos for promotional purposes. Most use such photos on their websites. If this is a concern for you, discuss an alternative arrangement with the photographer.

CHECKLIST 9
Photography Contract Details

[ ] Photography fee.

[ ] Deposit amount.

    [ ] Date of deposit payment.

[ ] Overtime fees, per hour.

[ ] Travel fee.

[ ] Cancellation fees.

[ ] Refund policy.

[ ] Final payment due date.

[ ] Total cost, including taxes and fees.

[ ] Date (and day of week) of wedding.

[ ] Booking client's name (usually the to-be wife or husband), address, email address, and phone number.

[ ] To-be spouse's name, email address, and telephone number.

[ ] Couple's future address (if different from booking client's address).

[ ] Name and cell phone number of a person the photographer can call on the wedding day in the event a complication arises.

[ ] Time of wedding ceremony.

[ ] Time of reception start.

[ ] Date of rehearsal (if photographer will shoot the rehearsal).

[ ] Locations, including addresses, where photography is to take place:

    [ ] Wedding day preparation location.

[   ]   Ceremony location.

[   ]   Portraits location.

[   ]   Reception location.

[   ]   Opportunities for candid photography, locations, and times:

    [   ]   Wedding day preparation location.

    [   ]   Ceremony location.

    [   ]   Portraits location.

    [   ]   Reception location.

[   ]   Services:

    [   ]   Still photographs.

    [   ]   Video.

    [   ]   Scrapbook.

    [   ]   Prints and framed prints.

    [   ]   Wedding album.

    [   ]   Number of images to be provided to client.

    [   ]   Format (negatives, digital files) of images to be provided.

    [   ]   Due date for photographer to provide images to the client.

[   ]   Shot list.

[   ]   Flash photography, if applicable:

    [   ]   Permitted times and locations.

[   ]   Attire of photographer(s) and assistants.

[   ]   Other services required:

    [   ]   Second photographer for ceremony.

    [   ]   Fee for second photographer.

7

Choosing a Florist

Color is a very important aspect of your wedding. Not only do the colors you choose beautify every part of your wedding, they can unify the entire event. Your palette is a selection of colors that you will choose for the flowers, bridesmaids' dresses, groomsmen's ties, and reception table decorations. You want to keep your color choices to two or three. A handy trick is to make a trip to a paint store and use the paint chips to choose colors and match them for selecting a perfect palette with minimal effort.

Once you've selected your palette, you will know which colors you want to feature in your wedding flowers. You don't need to recreate the Gardens of Versailles to compose a floral ambience to surround your wedding events with beauty. However, you do need to find the right florist, who can make your dreams come true while staying within your budget.

1. Visualize: What Looks Gorgeous to You?

Do some research to refine your vision of your wedding day flowers. Browse through wedding magazines, and social media and florists' websites to see what appeals to you. Remember that in many cases, these images should serve as inspiration only — typically, they show very expensive floral designs. Gather photos of the floral arrangements that inspire you, and the flower types that appeal to you, and bring them with you when you meet with the florists. Magazine pages and electronic images on your tablet, phone, or laptop will help the florist understand what your vision is, and how your vision can be made into reality, within your budget.

Availability and price of specific flowers varies by the season. Some blooms are only available in spring, and not in late summer, for example. Your florist will know what's in season at the time of year you'll be married, and what the prices are for particular flowers at that time. Carnations are a popular cost-cutting choice, as they're less expensive than many other blooms, and can be beautiful in dense, single-color arrangements.

Typically, a mid-priced florist will charge the following:

- $100 and up for a bridal bouquet.
- $40 and up for bridesmaids' bouquets.
- $10 and up for boutonnieres.
- $15 and up for corsages.
- $35 and up for reception centerpieces.
- $15 and up for small vases to hang on chairs along the ceremony aisle.
- $200 and up for altar urns.

For an additional cost, many florists will provide decor services such as lighting and linens. Floor-length table linens add a fancy touch, and can provide ambience that reduces the need for additional decoration.

Remember that most florists charge a rental fee for vases, urns, and decorative items used to hold flowers and decorate the venues.

1.1 Maximize: Flourishes of beauty

For every giant bridal bouquet in the glossy magazines there's a smaller bouquet of equal beauty. You don't have to go big to go beautiful! Look for a florist whose work you love, and find out what his or her prices are for smaller-scale floral creations. A good florist can create astonishing loveliness without making a bouquet that will leave the bride with a sore arm and depleted budget! You can apply the minimalistic approach across the board, from the ceremony to the reception.

Understatement works, and when it works well, it has a powerful impact. Well-placed decorative flourishes can bring a room together, and create an atmosphere of beauty that will surround your guests. Greenery magnifies the effect of flower arrangements, and costs much less than flowers. Ask your florist to recommend ways to use greenery instead of flowers for arrangements, and for room decor.

If you plan ahead for it, you can repurpose your ceremony flowers for your reception. Altar urns can be moved to the reception venue. Hanging arrangements from chair backs, if in vases, may be used as cocktail-table or guest book table arrangements, or hung on the back of bridal party chairs. Bridesmaids' bouquets can be placed around the cake for color. Keep in mind that greenery and flowers wired to arches or chuppahs will be difficult and time consuming to reuse.

Low floral centerpieces are less expensive to make — because of both flower cost and labor time — and allow for freer table conversation. For an evening reception, small candles around centerpieces add a romantic touch to the reception atmosphere, at very little additional cost.

Tip: Using larger tables reduces your floral costs by cutting the number of centerpieces required. For couples on extremely limited budgets, single beautiful flowers in small vases can serve as centerpieces for a fraction of the cost of conventional centerpieces. Another alternative to centerpieces is glass bowls holding water and floating blooms, with greenery for accents.

2. Strategize: Going Solo

It's quite possible to cover your basic floral needs for a considerably lower price than what you would pay a florist. Major warehouse stores often carry inexpensive floral arrangements, including centerpieces. Flower shops, and online vendors, sell lovely bouquets and centerpieces that aren't specifically intended for brides and weddings — they're usually described as being for "any occasion" — and are therefore usually priced much lower.

If you're inclined to make your own arrangements, you can design and create your own wedding flowers — possibly with the help of family and friends. There are reputable floral supply companies with online catalogs that include loose flowers, and arrangements, which can be delivered. Shops also sell wedding-specific flowers, such as boutonnieres and corsages.

If you wish to really go solo, you can reduce costs significantly by creating your own wedding flower arrangements. Consider the following options:

- Buy a book or borrow one from the library on flower arranging.

- Watch online tutorials.

- Order flowers and greenery online, or buy them in a shop, along with florist's tape, ribbons, and pins, to make your own bouquets and boutonnieres.

- Model your creations on photos you've found in bridal magazines and on the Internet.

- Check Pinterest for ideas. You'll find an exceptional selection of wedding photos to peruse on Pinterest, but keep firmly in mind that many of the photos of floral designs are widely pinned because they're world-class designs by some of the most expensive florists in the world, using the most costly flowers money can buy! Take inspiration, but be realistic about what you can afford.

- Order flowers and greenery online, or buy them in a shop, and do your own decorative arrangements, using large mason jars or inexpensive vases full of flowers for centerpieces, and smaller mason jars or vases for smaller arrangements.

- Place your arrangements at both the ceremony site and the reception location. Vases full of flowers can be attached to chairs closest to the aisle at the ceremony.

- Use greenery because it is less expensive than flowers, and can add to the beauty of flower arrangements while reducing the cost.

- Contract with a florist for minimal service such as a simple bridal bouquet, and small bouquets and boutonnieres for the wedding party.

Important: Making your own flower arrangements that look beautiful, and hold together, is far from as easy as it looks. You'll need to practice far enough in advance that if you discover you can't create what you envision, you'll have time to hire a florist. You'll need to schedule time to do this within two days of the wedding. Remember to store them in a very cool place; keep in mind that interior temperatures of home refrigerators can vary by position inside the fridge, and there may be a risk flowers will freeze and be spoiled.

3. Visualize: What You Need to Know before Contacting the Florists

By using Worksheet 5 (Top 5 Vendor Choices), from Chapter 3, you will know which florists you want to contact. Once you have decided the date of your wedding, your first question should be whether or not the florist is available to create floral arrangements for your special day. This way you can rule out a florist quickly if he or she is unavailable.

Before you call, gather the following information because the florist will need to know the answers:

- Date (and day of week) of ceremony and/or reception.

- Start time of ceremony and/or reception.

- Wedding and reception location.

- Budget for flowers.

- Flower arrangements needed (see Worksheet 7 at the end of this chapter).

Checklist 10 provides you with questions to ask the florist.

CHECKLIST 10
What You Need to Ask the Florist

[ ] Are you available on our wedding date?

[ ] How much experience do you have with creating wedding flowers?

[ ] Are you able provide the items I require, including floral arrangements and decorations, for a price within my budget?

[ ] Do you provide linen rental (if required)?

[ ] Do you charge a travel fee? If so, how much?

[ ] What are your installation fees?

After your phone calls, make your top pick and meet with him or her. Ask any further follow-up questions you may have. If the discussion produces satisfactory results, obtain a contract from the florist. Remember to call the florist at least one month in advance of the wedding to confirm the details of flowers and services.

If the meeting doesn't result in an agreement to proceed, visit the next florist in your list.

4. Scrutinize: Understanding the Florist's Contract

Your contract with your florist must include specific descriptions of the goods and services to be provided. Most florists' contracts also give them the right to substitute similarly priced alternatives to flowers if the flowers specified in the contract end up unavailable by the time of the wedding.

The contract will have a cancellation clause that specifies how much of your deposit or payment you would lose by canceling the contract, based on the amount of time before the wedding that you canceled. The deposit can be as high as 50 percent, and often the full amount is due 30 days before the wedding date.

Checklist 11 will help you itemize what details should be included in your contract with the florist. Worksheet 7 will help you keep track of the floral arrangements you need for your big day.

Worksheet 7
Flower Arrangements Needed

Item	Description	Quantity
Bouquets:		
Bride		
Maid of Honor		
Bridesmaids		
Flower girl(s)		
Bouquet for tossing		
Flowers for hair:		
Bride		
Maid of Honor		

Worksheet 7 — Continued

Bridesmaids		
Flower girl(s)		
Corsages:		
Bride's mother		
Groom's mother		
Boutonnieres:		
Groom		
Best Man		
Groomsmen		
Bride's father		
Groom's father		
Ceremony:		
Altar		
Aisle chairs		
Entrance		
Flower petals		
Non-floral decor items		
Reception:		
Head or sweetheart table centerpiece		
Other table centerpieces		
Guest book table		
Cake table		
Buffet table		
Non-floral decor items		
Other Venue Decor:		
Flowers/Greenery		
Lighting		
Linens		
Candles		
Lanterns		

[ ]   Date (and day of week) of wedding and/or reception.

[ ]   Ceremony time.

[ ]   Reception time.

[ ]   Location of wedding site.

[ ]   Location of reception site.

[ ]   Florist set-up time for reception.

[ ]   Florist set-up time for ceremony.

[ ]   Time and location of any deliveries before the wedding day.

[ ]   Florist cell phone number.

[ ]   Client cell phone number.

[ ]   Name and cell phone number of alternate person the florist can call on the wedding day in the event of an issue.

[ ]   Flower arrangements needed and description.

[ ]   Total cost, including delivery and installation fee, taxes and other fees:

    [ ]   Delivery and installation fee.

    [ ]   Deposit amount.

    [ ]   Due date of deposit.

    [ ]   Overtime fees, per hour.

    [ ]   Travel fees.

    [ ]   Cancellation fees.

    [ ]   Refund policy.

    [ ]   Final payment due date.

Finding a Music Provider

Music, live or recorded, creates the ambiance for both the wedding ceremony and the reception. The music for each of those events is often different. Before you start your discussions with the music providers, you need to make some decisions such as the wedding date and location, as well as the type of music and specific songs you want played at your wedding and reception.

Your options for ceremony and reception music include the following:

- Use prerecorded music and a rented or borrowed sound system.

- Hire a DJ.

- Hire musicians.

- Hire a band.

You may wish to have live music for the ceremony (which may be less expensive than live music for the reception because the duration of the service is shorter) and a DJ for the reception. Or a DJ can provide music for both events.

For some brides and grooms, live music is essential for the ceremony. A trio or quartet is not necessary for creating a lovely atmosphere appropriate to the occasion, and in keeping with your vision of your wedding day. In fact, the sound of a single instrument has a particular beauty that is quite suitable for many weddings. Consider a guitarist, cellist, violinist, or harpist — or even, depending on your preferences and wedding-day vision, a trumpet player or saxophonist!

For a ceremony, a trio or quartet of live musicians generally starts at around $500, but single musicians may provide ceremony music starting at around $100 (harpists are usually more). For a reception, live bands usually start at about $2,000, while DJ prices start at around $300.

Your music provider should be as well-versed as possible in wedding performances, and can use the sound system to direct guests as necessary during the ceremony and reception.

1. Scrutinize: Finding the Talent

There are plenty of talented budding musicians and DJs out there, and they will often work for much lower prices than established performers. Local music schools, conservatories, colleges and university music departments, music academies, DJ academies, and private music teachers can help you find solo performers, music groups, and DJs who are either immersed in music studies or freshly out in the professional performing world.

Keep in mind that performers who are just starting out may not know their way around weddings, or business practices. If you go this route, here's what to look for in a prospective music provider:

- Has wedding experience.

- Has a business card.

- Can provide references.

- Can provide a demo CD or DVD (for DJs, a DVD with a video promo reel) or an electronic demo file.

- Has a repertoire that fits your musical tastes.

- Has a wardrobe that fits your needs.

- Returns calls and emails promptly.

Just as you look at portfolios for photographers and taste a caterer's sample menu, you need to hear what a music provider sounds like before you hire. Remember to check references and online reviews.

2. Strategize: Do-It-Yourself Music

If someone among your friends and/or family has some expertise in portable sounds systems or DJing, playing your own selection of pre-recorded music at the ceremony and reception can bring considerable cost savings, but this may add a degree of risk. A DJ highly recommended by a friend or family member could turn out less than competent — or, worse, by being obnoxious and arrogant with a microphone in hand — despite having musical talent. A DJ who's a member of the family could become party to a family dispute, potentially causing all kinds of problems. Or the DJ may have talent, and a great demo disc, but own substandard equipment.

The Bridal Association of America sells CDs of popular wedding songs for less than $20. You can also find lists of wedding songs on-line, and download them from music services. You can follow the same process for reception music — and ensure only your favorite songs are played!

If you're having a cocktail hour, you can have the venue play music over the public address system, if available, during the cocktail hour, and you can reduce costs by having your reception music provider start later.

3. Visualize: What You Need to Know before Contacting Music Providers

By using Worksheet 5 (Top 5 Vendor Choices), from Chapter 3, you will know who you want to contact about music. Once you have decided the date of your wedding, your first question should be whether or not the music provider is available for your special day. This way you can rule out unavailable providers quickly.

Before you call, gather the following information because the music provider will need to know the answers:

- Date (and day of week) of ceremony and/or reception.
- Start time of ceremony and/or reception.
- Finish time of ceremony and/or reception.
- Hours of service needed.
- Wedding and reception events requiring music.

- Whether you will have live or recorded (DJ) music for your wedding ceremony and/or reception.

Checklist 12 provides you with a list of questions to ask the music provider. By printing the checklist from the download kit, you can make notes as you are talking to the person on the phone.

After your initial phone calls, make your top pick and meet with him or her. Ask any further follow-up questions you may have. If the discussion produces satisfactory results, obtain a contract from the music provider. Remember to call the music provider one month in advance of the wedding to confirm details of services.

If the meeting doesn't result in an agreement to proceed, visit the next music provider on your list.

4. Scrutinize: Understanding the Music Provider's Contract

Your contract with the music provider, as with other vendor contracts, will likely need to be much more detailed than the music provider's standard boilerplate contract. You need to make sure the contract specifies exactly when the music will begin and end for the ceremony, reception, or both.

Keep in mind that you're hiring this person, or group, to provide the soundtrack to your momentous event, so it's important that the soundtrack contain all the songs you want, and that the contract specifies those songs. It may also be important that certain songs not be played; if so, a "do not play" list must be included in the contract as well. Checklist 13 gives you details of what should go in a contract with a music provider.

CHECKLIST 12
What You Need to Ask the Music Provider

[   ]   Are you available on date of wedding?

[   ]   What is your price for the required services?

[   ]   How many wedding performances have you done?

[   ]   Can you supply the required types of performers?

[   ]   Will you respect a "do not play" list?

[   ]   What are your travel fees?

[   ]   Can you provide three references that I may contact? (When you contact the references, ask for both their positive and negative feedback in working with the music provider.)

[   ]   Can you play all the songs I require for the ceremony?

- During guest arrival: _____
- When the bride walks down the aisle: _____
- When the groom walks down the aisle: _____
- After the bride and groom are married: _____
- When the couple walks down the aisle: _____

[   ]   Can you play all the songs I require for the reception?

- First dance: _____
- Bride and father dance: _____
- All guests dance: _____
- Type(s) of music other than chosen songs: _____

CHECKLIST 13
Music Provider Contract Details

[   ]   Client's name (usually the to-be wife or husband), address, email address, and phone number.

[   ]   To-be spouse's name, email address, and telephone number.

[   ]   Name and cell phone number of person music provider can call on the wedding day in the event a complication arises.

[   ]   Date (including day of week) of wedding.

[   ]   Time of wedding ceremony.

[   ]   Location of wedding ceremony.

[   ]   Time of reception start.

[   ]   Location of reception.

[   ]   Time of reception end.

[   ]   Description of music services for the ceremony:

    [   ]   Number of musicians/DJs.

    [   ]   Instruments to be played.

[   ]   Description of music services for the reception:

    [   ]   Number of musicians/DJs.

    [   ]   Instruments to be played.

[   ]   Name(s) of performers, and alternates in case of emergency.

[   ]   Hours of service:

    [   ]   Ceremony.

    [   ]   Reception.

[   ]   Set-up time:

    [   ]   Ceremony.

    [   ]   Reception.

[   ]   Music start time:

    [   ]   Ceremony.

    [   ]   Reception.

[   ]   Music end time:

    [   ]   Ceremony.

    [   ]   Reception.

[   ]   Song list.

[   ]   Do not play list.

[   ]   Specified wardrobe for performers, if any.

[   ]   Scheduling and duration of breaks for music providers.

[   ]   Responsibility for furniture required for musicians, if any.

[   ]   Responsibility for amplification, if any.

[   ]   Total cost, including taxes and fees:

    [   ]   Deposit amount.

    [   ]   Cancellation fees.

    [   ]   Refund policy.

    [   ]   Overtime rates.

[   ]   Final payment due date.

9

Selecting Your
Wedding Attire and Rings

It's no secret that brides want to look beautiful and grooms want to look handsome on their special day. This makes the wedding attire for the bride and groom the most important factor in creating the look the couple wants. The attire doesn't need to cost a fortune to create the wardrobes that will help the bride and groom look their best — on the wedding day, and forever after in the wedding photos.

Speaking of forever after, the wedding rings of the bride and groom will remain a symbol of love, and reminders of the couple's commitment to each other. So the wedding bands are important, but as with the wedding wardrobe, they need not be costly to be beautiful.

1. Visualize: Your Wedding Dress

Your dress will be a focal point for the entire wedding; not only because you, the bride, are one of the two most important people in the event, but because the wedding gown carries a deep significance as a symbol of beauty and love.

The gown, veil, and jewelry should fit with the overall wedding style, and its color should harmonize with your palette of colors, to create a beautiful aesthetic, and help unify the wedding into a lovely and expressive whole. The location of your ceremony can play a role in your choice of dress style; for example, if you're getting married in an open field, you may want a less formal dress than if you're getting married in a church of great grandeur.

Technology is your friend in the search for a gorgeous and affordable wedding dress. The Internet will help you come up with a clear vision of the style of dress you want, and it will help you find the vendor that will provide what you're looking for at a price within your budget. Be careful because some unscrupulous online wedding dress vendors show photos of beautiful dresses, but ship out poor-quality dresses that leave soon-to-be brides in tears.

Photos of wedding dresses of every style, and at every price, can be found by the thousands in wedding magazines, on wedding-industry websites, and in social media. Use these pictures to identify, as specifically as possible, the style you want for your dress; this will greatly speed up the shopping process! Clip photos from magazines, and copy photos onto your phone, tablet, or laptop, and take the pictures with you when you are looking at dresses in the wedding shops.

Warning: You're going to see some beautiful dresses that cost more than many people earn in a year. You can get style and color ideas from these images, but you must not expect to fit one of the world's most expensive wedding dresses into your budget!

You have, essentially, six choices when it comes to acquiring your wedding gown, which the following sections discuss.

1.1 Custom made

Custom-made gowns can be an expensive choice. In general, unadorned custom wedding gowns start at around $300, with more elaborate gowns costing upwards of $2,000. Fabric choice (e.g., silk is far more expensive than satin) and length of the train are primary factors in the pricing. Look for a seamstress or tailor who has substantial experience with wedding gowns, and a portfolio showing work you admire.

1.2 Off the rack

Off-the-rack options are plentiful, and your Internet research should direct you to the right places to shop. At many department stores, you can find basic, unadorned wedding dresses starting at about $150 at the higher-end department stores, and less than $100 at discount department stores. There are thousands of options online in the same price ranges.

If you're shopping for a gown in bridal salons, you can save yourself considerable time by calling salons ahead of time to make appointments so you receive prompt, personalized assistance.

It's also definitely worth taking a look at sample gowns that bridal salons offer for sale. You may find one that fits your style, and doesn't require heavy alteration to look perfect on you. Salons may also have dresses at clearance prices, and you may find one you like that's in or close to your size. Note that bridal gowns often go on sale in late spring and early winter.

Specialty wedding shops tend to charge premium prices for gowns and accessories. A white or an ivory evening gown — or even prom dress — from a department store or smaller shop can cost much less than buying a wedding dress from a bridal shop, and may even require less alteration.

Be aware that an off-the-rack dress that requires significant alteration to fit you can end up costing more than a custom-made dress — alterations can easily add $200 to $500 in costs.

1.3 Gently used

One of the best ways to reduce wedding gown cost is to buy one that has been worn before. If you're set on a particular designer, this may be the only way you can afford the dress. The fact that you will only wear the dress once, and that a previously worn gown is, basically, recycled and an environmentally sound choice, can add to the appeal of this option. Nobody has to know you weren't the first to wear the dress, unless you tell them!

Bridal consignment shops can be found both online and in physical locations. You can also find pre-worn dresses on "auction" websites such as eBay — narrow your search results and save time by including the size when you search. Craigslist is another place to look — and searches will turn up results for both private sellers and companies and shops that may be selling wedding gowns for clearance prices.

Plenty of gently used dresses are on sale for less than $100, but be mindful that if your dress needs major alterations, your total price could climb rapidly.

1.4 Rental

The rental option is becoming increasingly popular, and it is also a "green" choice. By renting, you can increase the quality while decreasing the cost to a fraction of the purchase price.

Typically, wedding gown rentals start at around $75 and increase in price according to the value of the gown being rented. Some shops that rent dresses allow alterations, but some don't, in which case it may be more difficult to find one that fits you perfectly.

1.5 Borrowed

Do you have a close family member or dear friend who still has her wedding dress? You may find that such a person in your life was close to your size when she was married, and wore a gorgeous gown. Brides who are able to take advantage of an opportunity such as this receive the double benefit of saving money, and wearing a symbol of a close family or friendship connection.

1.6 Non-traditional gown

Increasingly, brides are choosing an economical wedding dress option that opens up a world of possibilities. A traditional wedding dress can be exceptionally beautiful. A non-traditional dress or gown can be equally lovely and can cost significantly less, and lets the bride choose the style and color she loves best. The dress can be white, pink, blue, green, saffron, or even red! Style choices are limitless. The bride can choose a dress to match the season. The bonus being that the dress, unlike a traditional wedding gown, can be worn again in the future. Cost savings can be significant: A savvy shopper can find a lovely dress for as low as $50!

2. Visualize: Bridal Accessories — Veils and Shoes

Veils come in all styles, lengths, and prices, and while those at the high end are often particularly stunning, you should have no problem finding a beautiful veil that won't add a great deal to your wedding attire budget. As with wedding dresses, you can find a huge selection that can be ordered online (watch out for unscrupulous purveyors), or buy yours in a bridal salon or consignment shop. It's also possible to rent a gorgeous veil.

One of the most effective ways to save money when buying your wedding shoes is to look elsewhere than in bridal salons, where they're often premium priced. You can shop online, and in consignment shops. It's possible to have some shoes dyed to match a dress, but certain leathers aren't possible to dye, and shoe dye jobs may run if exposed to water because of rain or wet grass.

Important: Once you buy your shoes, make sure you wear them a couple times a week for several weeks before your wedding. You must break in your shoes, or you risk suffering severe pain and blisters on your wedding day!

3. Strategize: Hairstyle and Makeup

The bride, of course, not only wants to look fantastic on the day of her wedding, she wants to look fantastic for all the years ahead —in the wedding pictures!

Most brides will want to have a stylist do their hair for the big day, and many brides also hire a makeup artist. However, some brides have talented friends and family members who can style their hair and/or do their makeup for the wedding.

Often, brides want their hairstyle and makeup to give them a special look, appropriate to the importance of the event. However, a bride should take care not to depart too drastically from her everyday appearance, with a hairstyle and makeup that make her look quite different. Brides, you want a beautiful you, but you still want you!

To ensure that hair and makeup styles have the bride looking her best — and feeling her best — it's vital that she do trial runs with whoever will be doing her wedding day hairstyling and makeup. She should bring her veil or hairpiece, and any accessories she'll wear on her wedding day. If either the bride's hairstylist or makeup artist seems painfully slow while working on the trial run, rest assured that the process will likely be equally slow on the wedding day, which could cause problems!

Here are some ideas for achieving savings on wedding-day hairstyling and makeup:

- Talk to the staff at makeup counters at department stores and shops — many of them freelance on the side, doing special events makeup.

- If there's a beauty school in your area, call and ask about any talented students who are already working in the hairstyling or makeup fields.

- If the bride is skilled with makeup, she can put on her wedding-day face herself.

- Find a hairstylist and makeup artist who will do the trial run free if you pay in advance for the wedding day work.

4. Visualize: The Groom's Attire

Obtaining the groom's attire is generally much less complicated and expensive than acquiring the bride's dress. While rented bridal gowns have only become trendy in recent years, grooms have generally rented a suit or tuxedo —or they may even use a suit or tux they already own. Tuxedo rental can start at prices as low as $50, and a new tuxedo starts at around $300.

Often, a groom who rents a tux or suit can take care of his wedding wardrobe needs at a single location — one-stop shopping! A reputable rental shop will be able to provide a bow tie or tie, cummerbund or vest, shirt, cuff links, and shoes. If the best man and groomsmen will be renting suits, it makes sense to use the same shop as the groom.

Beware: Quality and service vary widely among rental shops. It's very important that the groom, best man, and groomsmen, try on all the attire they plan to rent, to ensure it suits them and fits well.

5. Scrutinize: Receipts for Attire

When you buy or rent the bride's dress and the groom's tuxedo or suit, you may not receive a formal contract, but instead a receipt. In whatever form it takes, the document must specify the following:

- Wedding date.

- Customer phone number.

- Alternate contact phone number.

- Total cost.

- Payment schedule.

- Style (number and description).

- Customer pick-up date.

- Alterations to be performed.

- Accessories.

6. Visualize: Your Wedding Rings

You're going to be wearing your wedding rings for the rest of your lives, so you want to make sure you love them, and that they're well-made and durable. Of course, wedding bands can be absurdly expensive, but they can also be completely affordable. The best news is that any ring can be a wedding band — you just have to wear it on the proper finger!

It can be less expensive to buy wedding bands online, but make sure you're able to quickly and easily return them for a full refund if they're not satisfactory.

Here are some ways to reduce the cost of your wedding rings:

- Opt for lower-karat gold. Often, there's little difference apparent to the eye, and because lower-karat gold has a higher proportion of alloy, it's more durable, and will wear more slowly.

- Consider rings made of less-expensive metals such as silver, titanium, palladium, tungsten, or stainless steel.

- Choose vintage or antique rings, which are often beautiful and full of character, as well as economically priced.

A note about the ring bearer: These days, having a child, usually a small boy, carry the rings (or replica rings) down the aisle to deliver at the altar has largely gone out of style. Nowadays, couples wishing to have children participate in the ceremony usually have them accompany another participant in the walk down the aisle.

If you do want to have a ring bearer, you'll need to obtain a ring pillow (craft shops are great places to find these, or you can order one online) and possibly inexpensive substitute rings if you don't wish to put your real rings in the care of a small child.

10
Wedding Party Gifts

Your bridesmaids and groomsmen are happy to be a part of your special day, to stand by you as living symbols of the richness of your friendships, of the ties that have supported you and built meaning into your lives. The traditional wedding gifts to the groomsmen and bridesmaids are a way to show your appreciation for what these important people mean to you.

Whether you give the same gift, or different gifts, to your bridesmaids and groomsmen is not important. What matters are the thought that goes into selecting the gifts and the act of giving them. That means you don't have to blow your budget on this portion of the wedding. You can easily find gifts that show your gratitude and don't cost a mint. Many items can be personalized with engraving or embroidering for little additional cost.

Traditionally, the bride's maid of honor and the groom's best man receive a special gift, different from those given to the other bridesmaids and groomsmen. From the following possibilities, you can select gifts for the bridesmaids and maid of honor, and the groomsmen and best man.

Bridesmaids' gifts:

- Bangles that come engraved with sentiments of friendship and gratitude.

- Small jewelry boxes.

- Small framed art prints.

- Artfully designed yoga mats.

- Cosmetics cases.

- Personalized or colorful makeup compacts.

- Engraved friendship vases.

- Personalized tote bags.

- Pendants.

- Charm bracelets.

- Personalized water bottles.

- Colorful flasks.

- Beach mats.

- Brooches.

- Earrings.

- Bath or spa robes.

- Personalized pens.

- Wet-bikini bags.

- Spa or manicure-pedicure gift certificates.

Groomsmen's gifts:

- Wine openers.

- Personalized pens.

- Personalized card holders.

- Personalized water bottles.

- Flasks.

- Money clips.

- Personalized decanters.

- Personalized beer growlers.

- Travel toiletries bags.

- Shaving sets.

- Personalized branding iron for barbecued meat.

- Pocket knives.

- Gym/sports bags.

- Personalized coolers.

- Multi-tools.

- High-tech flashlights.

- Engraved lighters.

You may have close family members or friends who have helped you with your wedding, or whose presence at your wedding is especially significant. You can express your gratitude after the event by giving them framed photographs of the wedding couple, or the couple with family or friends.

Invitations and Other Paper Products

It can be shocking to consider the amount of money you could spend on the paper products you'll likely require for your wedding. Fancy paper, deluxe engraving, and custom calligraphy for invitations, thank-you cards, reception-seating cards, programs, menus, and guest books look very nice, but cost a small fortune. For example, invitations can cost up to $10 each.

According to the Bridal Association of America, the average expenditure on wedding stationery tops $800! However, you can create beautiful paper goods for a fraction of that price. Many online services allow you to design your invitations, thank-you notes, and other wedding-related paper products. You can choose the fonts for the text, the color and design schemes, and the types of paper to be used.

Remember to include on your invitations a request that guests inform you of any dietary limitations so you can make provisions for vegans, vegetarians, dietary restrictions and allergies, and people with religion-based dietary constraints.

Here are the paper products you may need if you don't opt for a paper-free process:

- Save-the-date cards.

- Invitations.

- Envelopes for invitations.

- RSVP cards.

- RSVP envelopes.

- Ceremony program, if desired.

- Reception table-assignment cards, often called escort cards, with the name of each guest or names of each couple, and the table number at which they're to sit (cards are to be laid out alphabetically at the reception entrance).

- Reception table-number cards that go on each table.

- Reception meal menu, if desired.

- Thank-you cards to acknowledge wedding gifts.

- Guest book.

While many couples will feel it's essential to mail wedding invitations, there's no compelling reason to require invitees to RSVP through the mail. In fact, you can make it much easier on your invitees if you request that they respond electronically, by email. This way you save yourself the cost of the RSVP cards, envelopes, and stamps. You can also request that invitees respond by phone; however, you're going to be busy planning the wedding, and may not have time to take calls and to chat.

For invitees whom you know are not comfortable with email, handwrite your phone number on the invitation so they can easily reply. The cost-boosting practice of mailing save-the-date cards to give friends and family advance notice of your wedding and the date can easily be done electronically, via email or social media.

1. Strategize: A Paper-Free Process

It is the 21st Century, and although paper wedding invitations are traditional, you may not personally feel you need them. Many couples appreciate an opportunity to make a "green" choice by reducing or eliminating paper products. You can reduce costs for invitations to little or nothing by keeping the entire invitation-and-response process electronic.

Online, you can find free or low-cost services that allow you to design and electronically send wedding e-invitations, and your invitees can respond online. The electronic method gets a little touchier with regard to expressing gratitude for gifts, as mailed thank-you notes are still considered by many people to be the proper way to respond.

2. Minimize: The Cost of the Guest Book

Many couples are opting these days to forgo the traditional book for creative options. While you can find a classic guest book online or at a shop, other possibilities can add fun and meaning to your guest register.

Here are some possible alternatives to the traditional guest book:

- A photo of the bride and groom set in a large photo mat, either unframed or removed from the frame, so guests can sign the mat around the picture, and the couple can frame it after the wedding.

- A coffee-table book that has meaning for the couple, and space around photos that can be signed by guests.

- An item that has special significance to the couple, which can be signed by the guests, such as a softball mitt, canoe paddle, pair of skis, restaurant menu, or map.

Remember to have pens on hand that are suitable for writing on the surface you'll have the guests sign. Also note, you or the venue or caterer will need to arrange for a table on which to put the guest register — in whatever form it takes.

3. Minimize: The Cost of Wedding Invitations

You can send beautiful invitations for a relatively low cost. Online custom printing companies allow you to easily design your invitation, and obtain samples before you place your order.

As mentioned earlier, you can make it very easy for your invitees to respond, by requesting that they do so via email. For those who don't use email, you should add a handwritten note requesting they respond by phone. Remember to include the day of week and the date for the wedding, just to make double-sure there's no confusion.

The invitations have been traditionally bought and sent by the bride's parents, but many betrothed couples now do it themselves. Either way, the same process can be followed. If you've made hotel arrangements for out-of-town guests, that should be noted on the invitation.

Sample 1 shows an example of an invitation that the bride's parents are responsible for sending. Sample 2 shows a version of the invitation that the bride and groom are responsible for sending.

Sample 1

Invitation from Bride's Parents

Gerald and Jane Smyth
request the honor of your presence
at the marriage of their daughter

Mary Smyth

to

Michael Jones

on

Sunday, February 25, 20--

at

2:30 p.m.

at

Greenwoods Hall
7544 Winding Road
Minneapolis, MN 12345

and at the reception following

at

The Portal Restaurant
863 Happytrails Avenue
Minneapolis, MN 54321

Please RSVP by email to:
emailaddress@email.com, and if your answer is "Yes!"
please inform us regarding any dietary limitations.

For out-of-town guests,
we have made arrangements for reduced rates with the
Penderson Suites Hotel for attendees to our wedding.
For booking, call 555-555-5555.

Sample 2

Invitation from Bride and Groom

Mary Smyth and Michael Jones
request the honor of your presence
at their wedding

on

Sunday, February 25, 20--

at

2:30 p.m.

at

Greenwoods Hall
7544 Winding Road
Minneapolis, MN 12345

and at the reception following

at

The Portal Restaurant
863 Happytrails Avenue
Minneapolis, MN 54321

Please RSVP by email to:
emailaddress@email.com, and if your answer is "Yes!"
please inform us regarding any dietary limitations.

For out-of-town guests,
we have made arrangements for reduced rates with the
Penderson Suites Hotel for attendees to our wedding.
For booking, call 555-555-5555.

12 Official Business

In the Introduction of this book, you were asked to think of beauty, joy, fun, love, and memories you'll treasure together. Now it's time to think about the big day! But first, there are some bureaucratic matters to take care of. You are entering a legal union, and you need to go through a process to obtain a marriage license. The good news is, it's easy! This chapter will give you a simple checklist to follow to obtain your marriage license. You'll just need to find out what the specific process and requirements are for the area where you'll be married. You will need to find an officiant authorized to conduct marriages in the jurisdiction.

You'll need to make some transportation plans for your wedding day, and possibly hold a rehearsal. The following sections provide you with checklists and timetables you will need on your wedding day, as well as a detailed rundown of the typical order of events at the ceremony and reception. And, definitely not to be forgotten, the emergency kit for the bride!

1. The Wedding Officiant

When selecting the person who will conduct your marriage ceremony, you must decide whether you wish to have a justice of the peace or other licensed official, or a religious official. No matter what type of officiant you choose, that person must be licensed to conduct marriages in the jurisdiction in which you will marry — and the categories of authorized officiants varies by jurisdiction.

In many jurisdictions, religious officials authorized to conduct marriages are ordained ministers, priests, rabbis, or non-ordained members of religions who are licensed to perform marriages.

Nonreligious officials authorized to conduct marriages are typically justices of the peace and judges; some jurisdictions permit retired justices of the peace and retired judges to perform marriages.

It is crucially important that you hire a reliable, experienced officiant whom you know will show up on time for the rehearsal, if you have arranged for that person to conduct the ceremony rehearsal, and for the marriage ceremony. The officiant must also be relied on to know how the marriage certificate must be completed, signed, and witnessed (typically by the maid of honor and best man), and must submit the completed license, after the ceremony, by the required time.

Price of an officiant depends on where you're getting married (larger urban areas are often more expensive than smaller towns and rural areas). Other factors include the day of week, season, officiant's level of experience, and the services to be provided (whether the officiant will conduct the rehearsal ceremony, and whether he or she will conduct the ceremony according to a basic script required by law, or whether it will be customized to include special elements, such as a speech or poem provided by the bride and groom). On average, couples spend around $200 on an officiant. One way to save on the expense of an officiant is to hire him or her for the ceremony only, instead of having the person also conduct the rehearsal ceremony.

Your officiant must do the following:

- Regardless of whether he or she is a religious or nonreligious official, he or she must be authorized to perform marriages in the jurisdiction in which you will marry.

- Some religious officials who are not ordained by their order may be authorized to perform marriages, if they possess a license from the relevant authority.

- Receive from you the valid marriage license you have obtained.

- Know the requirements for the completion of the wedding license, including signatures, during the ceremony.

- Submit the completed wedding license to the relevant authority so the marriage will be officially registered; and do so within the allotted time.

- Attend the rehearsal dinner, if that is your agreement, and conduct the ceremony rehearsal.

- Arrive at the ceremony location with sufficient time to prepare for the ceremony.

- Conduct the marriage ceremony with professionalism and personal warmth.

1.1 The do-it-yourself officiant

In most areas of the United States, you can have a friend or family member become ordained online and act as your officiant. You'll save on the cost of an officiant, and you won't have to pay extra to include personalized touches such as poetry for the marriage service. **Note:** This is not a legal option in some states in the US, and not at all legal in Canada.

Your ordained friend or family member will still have to know the legal marriage requirements for the jurisdiction in which you will marry, ensure the proper paperwork is done and submitted on time to the relevant authority, and perform the marriage according to the law.

If you go this route, you must be sure the person you choose is capable and reliable enough to do the job.

2. Getting Your Marriage License

The process and requirements for obtaining a wedding license vary by jurisdiction. In the United States, marriages are registered at the county level, although the couple may then marry anywhere within the same state. In Canada, marriages are registered at the provincial or territorial level. To find out what the specific requirements and processes are in the jurisdiction you plan to marry, you must obtain that information from the county or province. This information should be available online.

In some jurisdictions, the license is issued immediately on acceptance of the application. Some jurisdictions require a waiting period — usually three to five days — between buying and receiving the marriage license. Some jurisdictions providing a license immediately impose a waiting period before the marriage can take place, typically one to three days.

Your marriage license becomes valid once it has been signed at the marriage ceremony, typically by the bride and groom, witnesses, and officiant. The officiant is responsible for submitting the completed license form to the relevant authority. You will receive a certificate of marriage that is for your records. An official marriage certificate can be obtained from the relevant authority after the officiant has returned the forms and the authority has officially registered the marriage.

Checklist 14 tells you what you need to obtain your marriage license.

CHECKLIST 14
Obtaining Your Marriage License

[ ] Planned date of wedding.

[ ] Government-issued photo identification for each member of the couple (check with the jurisdiction to find out what documents are accepted).

[ ] Birth certificates for each member of the couple.

[ ] If one or both members of the couple have been divorced, or had a marriage terminated through death or annulment, you will need the court documents showing the final judgment of divorce or marriage termination. (Some jurisdictions only require you to know the date and location where a divorce or an annulment was registered.)

[ ] Required fee (some jurisdictions accept only cash and checks, not credit cards).

[ ] Blood test (if required).

[ ] One or both of the people to be married, depending on whether the jurisdiction requires one or both members to be present to apply for the marriage license.

3. The Wedding Rehearsal

No matter how detailed a rehearsal you have planned — from a casual get-together of the wedding party to a full run-through of the ceremony — choosing a free or inexpensive location, and serving tasty but inexpensive food, are key to keeping the rehearsal from adding significantly to your costs. This is a perfect event for a private home, as it typically involves mostly the wedding party and close family members. Home cooking can be an option, including a BBQ or a pasta bar, or even take-out from a local restaurant.

The rehearsal should be a casual get-together that gives wedding party and family members, and the bride and groom, a chance to socialize together. If you've cut costs by hiring an officiant who will reduce her or his price if his or her attendance isn't required at the rehearsal, you can still take a practice run through nearly the entire ceremony — and leave some spontaneity for the main event!

4. The Wedding Ceremony

Your ceremony starts with the processional, and ends with the recessional.

Traditional processional:

- Music begins.

- Ushers seat guests and/or guests seat themselves.

- Officiant stands at the altar.

- Groom and best man come in from the side and stand at the altar. (If there is no ring bearer, best man may carry the bride's ring.)

- Bridesmaids and groomsmen walk in pairs down the aisle.

- Maid of honor walks alone, or with an usher, down the aisle. (If there is no ring bearer, she may carry the groom's ring.)

- Ring bearer walks down the aisle.

- Flower girl walks down the aisle.

- Any other children walk down the aisle.

- Bride walks down the aisle with her father, or other important male figure. (In today's weddings, brides often walk down the aisle with both parents, or only their mother, or alone.)

- Bride stands on the left of the officiant, groom stands on the right.

- Officiant gives invocation, greets guests, offers a prayer if it's a religious ceremony, introduces the couple, and announces the purpose of the event.

- Officiant may speak on the topic of matrimony.

- Officiant conducts the ceremony.

- Officiant explains the importance of wedding vows and asks the couple if they will marry each other.

- Bride and groom say, "I do"!

- Bride and groom exchange vows.

- Ring bearer provides rings, or best man hands the bride's ring to the groom and maid of honor hands the groom's ring to the bride,

- Bride and groom exchange rings.

- Officiant pronounces the bride and groom married, and offers blessing in some religious ceremonies.

- Bride and groom kiss!

- Officiant makes closing remarks.

Traditional recessional:

- Bride and groom face the audience and photographer.

- Bride and groom walk up the aisle.

- Flower girl and ring bearer walk up the aisle.

- Maid of honor, best man, groomsmen, and bridesmaids walk in pairs up the aisle.

5. The Wedding Day Transportation

For your wedding day transportation, the vehicles are less important than making sure the bride and groom and wedding party get to the ceremony and reception on time! The obvious choice for reducing transportation costs is by using your own vehicles, and with a limited budget, this can make sense.

Limousine charges tend to start around $50 an hour, and fuel or mileage charges, and gratuity, can add a fair amount to the cost. A six-person limo is usually the most economical choice, compared to larger limos of eight seats or more.

Rental vehicles can also be an option, if vehicles are required, or if the bride and groom want to upgrade their ride for the day. Someone close to the bride and groom with a snazzy car might be honored to provide chauffeur services on the wedding day.

Whichever means of transportation you choose, your wedding day transportation timetable, with drivers designated, will keep important timing and other details at hand, and also allow you to plan in advance how the bride and groom and wedding party will travel safely throughout your wedding events.

Important: Designate contacts between the male and female members of the wedding party so the bride's and groom's parties can contact each other as needed if and when the groups are separated.

Keep track of important times and transportation plans with this timetable in Worksheet 8.

Worksheet 8

Wedding Day Transportation Timetable

Bridesmaid contact with groom's party: _____

Groomsman contact with bride's party: _____

Activity	Time	Driver	Method of Transportation
Leave preparation site for ceremony:			
Bride and bridal party			
Groom and groomsmen			
Leave ceremony for reception or photography:			
Bride and bridal party			
Groom and groomsmen			
Leave photography site for reception:			
Bride and bridal party			
Groom and groomsmen			
Leave reception:			
Bride and groom			
Bridal party			
Groomsmen			

6. The Wedding Reception

While there's still a fairly standard procedure for wedding ceremonies, these days, receptions take all forms, and although many feature a set of shared events, the timing of each event varies from reception to reception. You may want some "special dances" but not others. You may want to cut the cake right after food service or during a break in the dancing. What's important is you know what sequence to follow. If you have a music provider, he or she needs to know what the order of events is in order to play the appropriate music. The music provider can make the necessary announcements to instruct guests about what's happening.

By using Worksheet 9, you can arrange the events in the order you want them to take place.

Worksheet 9
Reception: Order of Events

Number	Activity
	Cocktail hour
	Bridal party enters
	Food service
	Toasts
	Cake cutting
	First dance
	Father and bride dance
	Mother and groom dance
	Anniversary dance
	Bouquet/garter toss
	General dancing
	Other:

7. Additional Forms to Help You Stay Organized

Your maid of honor or good friend should carry a small emergency kit to take care of any wedding-day mishaps that may occur, from a headache to a torn gown. Checklist 15 itemizes the things you may need.

CHECKLIST 15
Wedding Day Emergency Kit

[ ] Buttons

[ ] Superglue

[ ] Small bottle of Tylenol, ibuprofen, or aspirin

[ ] Small hairspray

[ ] Mascara (possibly waterproof!)

[ ] Sewing kit

[ ] Eyedrops/contact lens solution

[ ] Kleenex

[ ] Band-Aids

[ ] Stain remover

[ ] Bobby pins

[ ] Safety pins

[ ] Earring backs

[ ] Deodorant

[ ] Baby powder

[ ] Gum or breath mints

[ ] Feminine hygiene products

[ ] Directions to reception from ceremony

[ ] Photography shot list

Worksheet 10 will help you keep track of the gifts received, from whom, and whether or not you have sent a thank-you note.

Worksheet 10
Gifts Received

Name	Item	Thank-You Note Sent

Worksheet 11, Wedding Party Contact List, will come in handy throughout your wedding preparation plans.

Worksheet 11
Wedding Party Contact List

Party Member	Name	Phone Number	Email Address
Made of Honor			
Bridesmaid			
Bridesmaid			
Bridesmaid			
Best Man			
Groomsman			
Groomsman			
Groomsman			
Usher			
Usher			
Flower Girl			
Ring Bearer			

You're well on your way to planning a wedding that will match your dreams of romance, beauty, joy, and fun. And you hold in your hand the means to accomplish that goal as easily, economically, and enjoyably as possible. Have fun, and good luck on your special day!

Download Kit

Please enter the URL you see in the box below into your computer web browser to access and download the kit.

www.self-counsel.com/updates/weddingbliss/15kit.htm

The download kit offers forms in MS Word and/or PDF format so you can edit as needed. It includes:

- Checklist and worksheets to help you plan your big day without a big budget.